W9-BFS-921

**LARGE
PRINT
EDITION**

**RANDOM
HOUSE**

ALSO AVAILABLE
IN RANDOM HOUSE LARGE PRINT

Living Faith
Sources of Strength

THE VIRTUES
OF AGING

Jimmy Carter

Published by Random House Large Print
in association with
The Ballantine Publishing Group
New York

Library of Congress Cataloging-in-Publication Data

Carter, Jimmy, 1924–
The virtues of aging / Jimmy Carter.
p.   cm.
ISBN 0-375-70460-4 (pbk. : lg. print)
1. Aging—Social aspects.
2. Aging—Psychological aspects.
3. Aging—Government policy.   I. Title.
[HQ1061.C354   1998b]
305.26—dc21   98-26244
                                                              CIP

Random House Web Address:
http://www.randomhouse.com/
Printed in the United States of America
FIRST LARGE PRINT EDITION

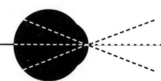

This Large Print Book carries the
Seal of Approval of N.A.V.H.

*To my father, Earl, my brother, Billy,
and my sisters, Gloria and Ruth,
all of whom died too young;
and to my mother, Lillian,
who demonstrated the virtues of aging.*

The Meaning of Virtue

In thinking about the book's title, Rosalynn and I discussed the meaning of the word *virtue* and decided that both basic definitions were applicable: "a particularly beneficial advantage" and "an inherent quality that is admirable." In other words, the virtues of aging include both the blessings that come to us as we grow older and what we have to offer that might be beneficial to others.

Acknowledgments

I'd like to thank my editor, Peter Gethers, and others who helped me with this manuscript: Nessa Rapaport, Dr. Ken Dychtwald, Dr. Bill Foege, Faye Dill, Dr. Steve Hochman, and my wife, Rosalynn.

With one exception, as noted, the quotations at the beginning of each chapter have come from the late Jimmy Townsend, my personal friend and a wonderful mountain philosopher, whose books and weekly columns have delighted southerners for many years.

Introduction:
I'm Old, but It's Good!

Even before leaving the White House, Rosalynn and I received a notice from the American Association of Retired Persons that we were qualified for membership, but we considered ourselves too young to face the stigma of senior citizenship. However, once back in Plains the point was to be driven home most firmly and clearly. We live 120 miles south of Atlanta and habitually drive back and forth to The Carter Center and to Emory University, where I am a professor. One morning we left our house quite early and stopped to eat breakfast in Thomaston, Georgia, about halfway to Atlanta. There were four of us in the car, and we all ordered about the same thing. But when the waitress brought my bill, I noticed that it was less than the others. Perhaps seeking credit for being an honest customer, I called her back and began to tell her that she had made a mistake. An older farmer, dressed in overalls, was sitting at a nearby table and apparently overheard my conversation. He looked over at us and called out in a loud voice, "Your bill ain't no mistake, Mr. President. Before eight o'clock they give free coffee to senior citizens."

A wave of laughter began at our table, and it still resonated through the restaurant as I paid my bill and hurried back to the car. For several weeks afterward, every time we approached Thomaston I knew that someone would say, "Why don't we stop here for breakfast? There's free coffee for some of us!"

In the years since returning home, Rosalynn and I have been through some severe tests and have struggled to find the best way to retain our self-confidence, evolve an interesting and challenging life, and build better relations with other people. As we've grown older the results have been surprisingly good.

The first time I fully realized how much our lives had changed was when I approached my seventieth birthday. In one of her hourlong special interviews, Barbara Walters covered all the aspects of my life, from the farm to submarines, from business to the governor's mansion, service in the White House, and from president back home to Plains. Then she asked me a question that required some serious thought: "Mr. President, you have had a number of exciting and challenging careers. What have been your best years?" After a few moments I responded with absolute certainty: "*Now* is the best time of all." She was surprised, and asked, "Why?"

I fumbled with some thoughts about time for reflection, spending more time with my family, and a chance to correct some of my former errors. Afterward I realized how inadequate my glib, thirty-second answer had been, and I discussed with Rosalynn how profoundly different—and pleasant—was the reality of our senior years.

This book is my expanded attempt, based on our personal experiences, to answer that question—to describe, in effect, the virtues of aging.

1

Kicked Out, Broke, but Fighting Back

*Experience is what you've got plenty of
when you're no longer able to hold the job.*

I was just fifty-six years old when I was involuntarily retired from my position in the White House. What made losing the job even worse was that it was a highly publicized event, with maybe half the people in the world knowing about my embarrassing defeat!

There were also some other problems that were especially troublesome for Rosalynn and me. Within a few days of the disappointing 1980 election, the trustee of my blind trust informed me that while I was president a lack of close personal management and a pervasive drought in the Southeast had cost us dearly. What had been our flourishing farm supply business was now more than a million dollars in debt.

We soon realized that there was no local market for a peanut buying point and farm supply business, and the community offered no real job opportunities for a family like ours. In order to pay what we owed, we faced the prospect of selling all our land, some of which had been in our family for 150 years, and perhaps taking out a mortgage on our only home. Even then, we had no assurance that we could raise enough cash to avoid an embarrassing bankruptcy.

Our despair was even more acute because we realized that our daughter, Amy, would soon be going off to school, leaving just the two of us alone. We would be left without the full and lively home that we had enjoyed with our children since we returned to Plains from the U.S. Navy in 1953.

There were other reasons as well why moving from Washington back to our home in Plains was not a pleasant experience. It was not easy to forget about the past, overcome our fear of the future, and concentrate on the present. In this small and tranquil place, it was natural for us to assume—like other retirees—that our productive lives were about over. Like many other involuntary retirees, we had to overcome our distress and make the best of the situation.

When one of our friends pointed out that more than a third of American men in my age group were retired, and that we could expect to live until we were eighty years old, I had one disturbing reaction: What was I going to do with the next twenty-five years?

We soon had a stroke of financial luck when a major agricultural firm decided at that time to expand their dominant position in the corn and soybean business to include peanuts. They bought Carter's Warehouse and six other similar sites in Georgia and Alabama to give them an adequate supply of their new product. In addition, I negotiated a contract with a publisher for my presidential memoir. The combined income helped us save our land and home.

We felt that nothing could replace the four more years that I had anticipated spending as the nation's president. Rosalynn was especially bitter and angry, unable to accept with equanimity the result of the 1980 election. I tried to think of some positive aspects of our lives, emphasizing that we had accomplished many things during my administration and had always done our best. But nothing I said or did could induce her to look to the future with any pleasure or confidence. For a while we just paused and contemplated our lives. To pass the time we laid down a floor in our attic, became reacquainted with our farmland, and jogged or took long bike rides through the countryside, stopping to visit at the homes of our friends of past years.

And then after a few weeks I was suddenly busy, with at least a year's work of writing my memoirs but only after reading—for the first time—the diary notes I had dictated each day while president. There were six thousand pages, and they brought back vivid memories, some exhilarating, some bittersweet. I guess anyone rereading one's own diary of bygone times would have similar feelings.

Rosalynn also decided to write her autobiography, and we slowly developed a more positive attitude. But we still didn't know what we would do with our remaining years.

One of our most valuable assets was a strong and supportive family. Most of them had been closely involved in our political campaigns and our work in the governor's mansion and the White House. All of them shared our political disappointment, but they, as well as Rosalynn and I, also benefited from being a close-knit team. Our two mothers and other relatives were still in Plains, which had been our only real home since we were born—and they helped make it easy for us to immerse ourselves in the affairs of the community. The following year I accepted a few speaking engagements, including one in Hawaii to the Young Presidents' Organization and a five-nation tour through Western Europe. I was surprised and encouraged by the friendly reception and the interest of the audiences in what I had to say.

It was not easy, but eventually we gathered enough courage to assess our talents, experience, and potential influence in affecting some of the social and political issues in which we were still interested. We finally made a major decision: to try to explore completely new commitments. We had done it several times when we were younger; why not now?

The first thing we had to do was to answer some basic questions that confront millions of other retirees: How could we accommodate the unpleasant circumstances that had been forced on us? What were our assets and abilities? What were the dependable factors in a good life, and how could we recognize and develop them? Was it at all possible for us to be as satisfied in the future as we had been during some of our most interesting, adventurous, and successful times? Did we have anything much to offer others in the years ahead?

Our answers at the time were not very encouraging. We didn't have jobs, we had made a commitment to live in Plains, neither of us had an advanced degree, and the existing book contracts seemed to cover all we would ever want to write. We did not yet understand that there were potential advantages ahead of us if we could only put to use the good advice we received, along with our personal assets, the support of our friends and family, and some courage and planning.

2

Fear of Aging:
But What Is "Old"?

*The scary thing about middle age is knowing
that you are going to outgrow it.*

Rosalynn and I were able to weather those days
successfully by developing completely new careers
that we had never anticipated. Both of us had offers
to become university professors, and we enjoyed
this challenge. We decided to establish The Carter
Center, within which we could pursue some of the
interests we had felt were interrupted when we
left the White House. Somewhat to our surprise,
our books were quite successful, and publishers re-
quested that we write additional ones. Still feeling
young and vigorous in our fifties and sixties, we

didn't think much about facing another transition in our lives.

But as we entered our seventies there was another potential threat to our happiness: the forced realization that both of us fit almost any definition of "old age." I guess it is unpleasant for any of us to face our inevitable gray or thinning hair and the tendency for our waistline to spread, especially when advancing years correspond to a reduced income. This brings a challenging but inevitable transition in our lives—from what we have been to a new type of existence as "senior citizens."

We are not alone in our worry about both the physical aspects of aging and the prejudice that exists toward the elderly, which is similar to racism or sexism. What makes it different is that the prejudice also exists among those of us who are either within this group or rapidly approaching it. When I mentioned the title of this book to a few people, most of them responded, "Virtues? What could possibly be good about growing old?" The most obvious answer, of course, is to consider the *alternative* to aging. But there are plenty of other good answers—many based on our personal experiences and observations.

It is clear that in some ways Rosalynn and I are not typical, having been the First Family of a great nation, a special status that cuts both ways, with benefits *and* liabilities. But in almost every aspect of life, our challenges have been similar to those of tens of millions of families who face the later years with a mixture of problems and opportunities, doubts and anticipation, despair and hope. We've had to address a common question: How could we ensure that our retired years would be happy, and maybe even productive?

In general, our own age determines whom we consider to be an old person. When I was in the navy and serving on my first ships, I assumed that officers and men who were retiring after twenty years of service were old, and those who held on for a maximum of thirty years were almost too set in their ways to deal with the changing realities of modern navy life. The first group was composed of men about forty-two years old, and the others were just ten years older! Even today, many men and women working as police, in military or other government service, and as employees in civilian jobs retire at about these same ages. To their juniors, they are old.

I guess a more general legal definition of *elderly* now would probably be sixty-five years of age or older, when Americans can begin to receive full Social Security benefits. It's interesting to note that Prince Otto von Bismarck, age seventy-four, first set the retirement age at seventy in Germany in 1889, when the average life expectancy was about forty-five. If we had the same twenty-year interval beyond present life expectancy, our government checks wouldn't begin coming until we were almost a hundred years old!

There have been profound changes in our lives during the last few decades—not just in how we live, but in how we work. When my father was born, in 1894, more than 75 percent of sixty-five-year-old men continued to work. Even when I resigned from the navy, in 1953, about half the able-bodied men of that age were still working. Just forty-five years later the proportion of sixty-five-year-olds still working has dropped to only 17 percent and is now holding steady. This figure is likely to increase as labor shortages continue and Social Security disincentives to work are removed.

Recently I noticed a poll in which Americans were asked, "What do you consider an optimum retirement age?" The average answer was fifty-four. Another question was, "At what age do you consider a person to be old?" The answers varied widely, but the average was seventy-three. So what happens during the twenty years or so between retirement and old age? Many of us just shift from full-time to part-time employment—either paid or as volunteers. To express this change succinctly, people used to continue working until they died; now we retire and then live nearly as many years as we were employed.

So then, when *are* we old? The correct answer is that each of us is old when we *think* we are—when we accept an attitude of dormancy, dependence on others, a substantial limitation on our physical and mental activity, and restrictions on the number of other people with whom we interact. As I know from experience, this is not tied very closely to how many years we've lived.

The status of older people in America has varied dramatically down through the centuries, mostly depending on their numbers, their property holdings and degree of self-reliance, and competition for jobs. Until the nineteenth century the few who survived were especially admired and respected. It was assumed that they were wise in managing their lives and, because they had survived, were also particularly blessed by God. It was even fashionable to *look* old; stylish men and women used white-powdered wigs to conceal their youthful blond, black, or auburn locks.

However, with the coming of the industrial revolution there was a shift from home and farm employment to work in factories, with more competition for jobs and a premium on workers who were stronger and more adept. Older citizens either could not compete or were seen as taking jobs from younger breadwinners. The result is that they came to be considered a burden on families and society in general.

The status of the elderly reached a low point during the Great Depression, when poverty was prevalent and jobs were scarce. When I was a child during that era, the value of members of a household was measured by their ability to work and earn income, which many of the older generation were unable to do. These nonproductive "elderly," some still in their fifties or sixties, were often a hardship, even an embarrassment, for a family. I remember the disgraceful status of old folks' homes, or "po' farms," where the old and destitute sat on the porch or, if able, scrabbled to produce a meager crop in adjacent gardens or fields. They were wards of the states or counties, forced to exist at a barely life-sustaining level.

Then in 1935 Social Security legislation was passed. This gave older people a subsistence income and, at the same time, removed them from competing in the workplace for scarce jobs. Since then the lives of older Americans have changed dramatically. Nowadays most of the elderly in rich industrialized countries like ours are relatively self-reliant and often able to contribute beneficially to their families and communities.

With this relative affluence and enormous political power, respect for us older people has reached a new high. A recent poll revealed that the American people share a surprising agreement on basic questions concerning retirees. Ninety-three percent of respondents believe that the elderly should be allowed to work as long as we wish. Eighty-two percent of Americans say that we have higher moral values than younger people, and 75 percent think wisdom comes with age. If the elderly are, indeed, blessed with wisdom, what does that word really mean? One definition of *wisdom* I like is "the ability to exercise good judgment about important but uncertain matters in life." Anthropological studies show that older people, influenced by the Great Depression, are more likely to believe that good lives are based on hard work, thrift, perseverance, belief in God, and stable families.

3

How Times Have Changed

Who did we blame our mistakes
on before computers?

People of my generation have experienced astonishing societal changes in our own lives and among our acquaintances. Rosalynn and I grew up in southwest Georgia, and our early lifestyle was more like that of our distant ancestors than that of our grandchildren. My family lived in relative isolation in a rural community; we didn't have electricity or running water in our house until I was fourteen years old. We shared all the necessary chores and were, therefore, a close-knit and secluded unit. My father worked six days a week until stricken with terminal cancer, and my mother, a registered nurse, did not consider herself to be retired until she was in her seventies. We children never questioned either their authority or their qualifications to manage our family. Nor did we envision the remarkable changes that lay ahead, both in interpersonal relationships and in the incredible technological innovations that would transform almost every aspect of American life.

My own attitudes were transformed dramatically as my career evolved. I planned my optimum career with confidence: to become an officer in the U.S. Navy. I would graduate from the Naval Academy, serve for a maximum of thirty years as a naval officer, and retire at the advanced age of fifty-two. Even after Rosalynn and I were married, we didn't change the basic plan. Perhaps, we thought, we'd raise two or three children (we didn't think about grandchildren) and then would live a relatively isolated life surrounded by other navy families. The only question concerning the distant future was where we would spend our declining years: in Hawaii or near Annapolis. We never really considered moving back to Georgia, and certainly not to Plains. I looked on my life span as divided into roughly two parts: the first was to be devoted to learning and advancing, and the second would be spent enjoying the privileges of high rank and well-deserved retirement. I didn't think much about how long this latter phase would be, but assumed ten or fifteen years if I was lucky.

Obviously my life has been quite different from what I anticipated, which is the experience of most Americans. Not only have my personal plans changed, but so have family relationships, the entire character of our society, and even what I considered to be immutable moral standards.

Many of the comparisons are based on my childhood observations. For instance, I grew up in a society where God's laws concerning marriage were strictly observed—at least officially. Before I went off to the navy, I never heard of anyone in the Plains community being divorced, and only widowed spouses ever remarried. Even as a child, however, I knew of married women who were living with men other than their husbands. Two husbands, who lived on farms within a mile of ours, fell in love with each other's wife and simply swapped families. The only change in their lives was that they quit going to church for a while. But now more than half of American marriages end in divorce, and the folks in Plains have tended to follow the trend.

Despite this, I've noticed that the attractiveness and the appeal of marriage don't seem to have changed very much. People who divorce are not against marriage, but only think theirs could be better; 80 percent of divorced persons remarry! One possible beneficial result is that divorces expand family circles. That's certainly true of ours. Two of our sons have remarried, so we have two extra families. And at a recent family reunion I noticed that one of my cousins had three daughters with nine husbands among them—and only one is still married.

There have been some other long-term changes that we now take for granted. Life expectancy at birth for Americans in most of the eighteenth and nineteenth centuries was in the low forties, similar to what it is today in the least developed nations. By 1900, this figure had increased to 47 years. But since then, with vaccines that prevent many formerly fatal diseases and with better medical treatment, the increase has been 110 days per year! Every day the average life expectancy of Americans increases by seven hours—that's approximately two days per week—and has now advanced to seventy-six years.

It should be remembered that the primary health improvements affecting longevity have occurred during childhood. Once people reach the age of fifty, their life expectancy is about the same as it has been for the past two hundred years. For instance, our first six presidents (Washington to John Quincy Adams) lived an average of 79.6 years; the last six who have died (Franklin D. Roosevelt to Richard Nixon) lived an average of 70 years. If we omit Kennedy, who was assassinated at an early age, the life span of the others is still only 74.8 years.

These increases in life span have had a vivid societal impact in the richer countries, with rapid shifts in the relative size of different groups. Population growth rates have been reduced significantly. Americans over sixty-five years of age now outnumber teenagers, and most of us are well and able to lead full and vigorous lives. During the past twenty-five years the number of people over the age of eighty-five grew almost six times more rapidly than the overall population. The fastest-growing group of all, however, is those over a hundred; in 1956 there were 2,500 centenarians, 25,000 in 1986, and by 2000 there will be 268,000!

(Note: The average American now has fewer children than parents.)

Whether we like it or not, these changes in longevity and retirement habits put new responsibilities on us. One thing we must do nowadays is prepare for long, drawn-out illnesses near the end of life. In the past, medical care was designed primarily to cure serious diseases, but with extended life spans have come chronic ailments such as Alzheimer's disease, arteriosclerosis, and osteoporosis. What used to be fatal heart and kidney diseases can now be treated successfully, sometimes for years, with expensive pacemakers, bypasses, dialysis machines, and even transplants. With the help of these medical procedures, at whatever age, we can expect to live relatively normal lives.

Patients suffering from more serious diseases, without hope of recovery, can be kept alive—even if barely—with mechanical substitutes for hearts, lungs, kidneys, and other vital organs. It seems that payments from governments and insurance companies make it financially beneficial for medical centers to keep us dying as long and as expensively as possible. Thirty percent of Medicare expenditures are during the last year of life, and often a substantial portion of the final expense falls on the surviving family members.

The distinction between these two types of treatment—returning us to a relatively active life or artificially prolonging a hopeless case—is arousing contentious moral debates, legal cases, arguments within families, and soul-searching by individuals. What should be done? Later I'll describe how my own family members have answered this question.

4

Looking Ahead: The Impending Crisis

*A joyous occasion is never quite as wonderful
as when it becomes a memory.*

When we had our three boys between 1947 and 1952, we didn't realize that they were part of what would be known as the "baby boom." Seventy-six million Americans were born during the eighteen years following World War II, creating an unprecedented surge in our nation's population. As our children have passed through different life stages, this enormous mass has drastically changed our society. Enrollment in high schools doubled between 1950 and 1975, and seven hundred new colleges were opened to accommodate a postsecondary student population that nearly tripled within ten years, from 3.2 million in 1965 to 9 million in 1975. Unemployment rates inched up as the labor force expanded more rapidly than available jobs. Then, for some reason, the birth rate in America reached its lowest point in history when the baby boomers began to reach childbearing age. Nowadays the persistently low unemployment rate is one indication of worker shortage, as baby boomers begin to retire or are laid off and their relatively few children enter the workforce.

The impact of the baby boomers, often called the "age wave," is not just a general social and political problem, but one that affects almost every individual family. Rosalynn and I can no longer just assess what is best for the two of us; we're coming to see more clearly that what is happening to our own generation is having a profound effect on our children and grandchildren. There is little doubt that this is leading to some competitions and conflicts that will confront our nation and other industrialized societies with the most important and controversial issue of the next millennium.

This financial confrontation has been predicted and deplored by our youngest son, Jeffrey, since he was a college student. He repeatedly asked how his age group, the baby boomers, could depend upon the Social Security system, Medicare, and other government programs for the aged. In those days, when I was governor and president, Rosalynn and I argued with him, stressing the confidence we had in our own government and its inevitable meeting of its responsibilities. Now, without major increases in funding sources and reductions in benefits for the elderly, I'm quite sure that Jeffrey was right.

After our three boys were born, Rosalynn and I had an on-again-off-again argument for fourteen years. I finally won, and Amy was born when our oldest son was twenty years old. Rosalynn was forty, and I realized that I would be a sixty-one-year-old PTA member. In effect, our immediate family members have grown up with three distinct experiences: the Depression years, the baby boom, and Generation X.

There is a sharp contrast between the concepts of our now middle-aged children and our own Depression-era fear of debt, commitment to savings, and cautious preparation for our later years. For us older persons, financial security is coming from accumulated savings, current employment, pension income, and government benefits. It seems that our attitudes are more compatible with those of Amy's and our grandchildren's generation than with those of our sons'. I asked a distinguished sociologist about this, and he agreed, explaining that the general attitude of baby boomers is different from that of any other generation he has studied. There is more of a "hand-to-mouth" attitude, a sense of uniqueness in historical terms, and a belief that, somehow, their needs will be met.

The fact is that programs for the elderly are facing a crunch that will force unpleasant choices on our children as they retire. The oldest baby boomers will begin receiving Social Security benefits in 2010, the beginning of an enormous wave. By the time our youngest grandson, Jamie, is a middle-aged wage earner, one in four Americans will be over sixty-five years old. Unless dramatic changes are made, the costs of Social Security, Medicare,

Medicaid, and federal pensions are projected to exceed *total* federal revenues by 2030. Belatedly, political leaders have begun to face this issue, which is destined to be the most important item on the domestic agenda throughout the developed world. Even now, in the United States, Europe, and Japan, it is replacing concerns about schools, housing, job training, even crime and a stronger defense.

Although general expectations about the future are still high, there is a growing skepticism among middle-aged Americans about the integrity of Social Security and Medicare. According to a recent nationwide poll among American young adults, 46 percent believe that UFOs exist, but only 28 percent think they can depend on Social Security when they retire, and less than 20 percent believe that Social Security will provide their main retirement income. Even so, most are not preparing for the future.

Our total U.S. savings rate is now hovering at only 2 percent of gross domestic product, with private savings at about 5 percent of earnings. Americans save less than a quarter as much as do the Japanese. Only 30 percent of American families are accumulating any long-term savings or pension benefits, while almost 45 percent are spending more than they earn. Most baby boomers (now between thirty-five and fifty-two years old) will have little if any savings when they retire. They are excessively inclined to depend on inadequate private retirement systems and government programs to meet their needs—benefits that are likely to be reduced below today's levels under pressures that are unavoidable.

Most political leaders have only recently acknowledged what many experts have long recognized: The future of the American Social Security system is in serious trouble. A few statistics will clarify the basic problem. When the program was first established, in 1935, there were about 40 wage earners supporting each retiree with their tax contributions. By 1990 there were only 3.3 workers for each recipient, and by 2010, when our sons are likely to begin leaving the workforce, only 2 people will be paying for the retirement and medical expenses of one senior citizen. By then, official projections are that the total federal cost of Social Security and Medicare will rise to 50 percent of the taxable payrolls of American workers.

Government spending on health care also has

been skyrocketing. When I was born, the government spent only about $1 a year per person for health care. In 1965 it was $100 (less than we spent per capita on defense); in 1975 it had risen to $1,000; and in 1995, $7,000. And all of this is before the mass of baby boomers reach retirement and Medicare age. Even now, many older Americans cannot afford either health care or the exorbitant costs of some insurance policies.

A substantial disparity already exists in government expenditures, with twelve times as many federal dollars being spent on an average retiree (above sixty-five) as on a child under eighteen. If we look at total federal government entitlements, even including welfare and Medicaid for the poor, households earning above $100,000 a year receive more than those making less than $10,000. Today, about half of the federal budget goes to pay for programs for the elderly. If basic changes are not made in entitlement programs, it has been predicted that by 2013 the entire federal budget will be going to pay for the elderly and for interest on the federal debt.

Do we deserve such special treatment? The fact is that I and more than a million other Social Security beneficiaries would be considered quite wealthy, while many of the Americans supporting us may be struggling to make ends meet. Compared to working parents between thirty-five and forty-four years old, the elderly have a per capita income that is 60 percent greater and three and a half times the net worth. At the same time, much of our income is not taxed. Nowadays, twice as many Americans under twenty are living in poverty as are those of us over sixty-five.

There is a special problem, however, with many aging Americans who are not wealthy, or whose retirement savings are expended several years before the end of life. This is of particular concern to older women, who become an increasing majority with advancing age. In the nursing home with Rosalynn's mother, there are twenty-seven other women and only six men. Sixty percent of Medicare recipients are female, and they use the benefits an average of fifteen years, compared to only seven years for men. The income of older women living alone is only about half that of men, they usually have smaller estates than men, and they become impoverished more quickly as their assets are frequently used to pay for nursing home care. When this occurs, Medicaid is the only remaining source of funding. There are now about 1.8 million Americans in nursing homes, at a total annual cost of $87 billion, of which Medicaid pays about half. Costs in the Lillian Carter Nursing Home in Plains are lower than this national average—about $2,500 per month plus an average of $250 extra for medicine. A room at Magnolia Manor in nearby Americus costs about $500 more.

At a recent family gathering, we had a hot discussion about the system of government payments, and as a beneficiary I had to acknowledge the inequities. A typical couple like Rosalynn and me will get almost $200,000 more in Social Security and Medicare benefits than we ever contributed to the funds. Current workers, including our children, are paying this difference, with their taxes going directly to us retired recipients. One of our daughters-in-law said, "I thought our Social Security taxes were going into something like a big safe, and would be waiting for us when we retire." Everyone laughed.

Actually, in order to claim a balanced budget, the president and Congress are applying hundreds of billions of dollars from Social Security taxes to the general fund. The taxes are more than enough to pay current benefits, and will be sufficient until around 2030, but after that date there will be about a 25 percent shortage of funding.

Social Security laws must change. Although Washington politicians are still justifiably reluctant to face the condemnation of the American Association of Retired Persons and the Gray Panthers by reducing these benefits, there is no doubt that *something* will have to change. A number of proposals are being assessed, including:

1. A means test, with reduced benefits for the rich
2. The taxing of all benefits for the wealthy
3. A reduced tax load on working families
4. A higher age to start receiving Social Security payments
5. A change in cost-of-living indexing
6. More opportunities for employment for the elderly
7. Encouragement of personal savings
8. Restraints on wasteful health-care procedures
9. Authorization for part of our taxes to be shifted to personal retirement accounts
10. Investment of some Social Security trust funds in the stock market

Such changes will be even more hotly contested as the seventy-six million baby boomers reach retirement age, when their greatly increased numbers will magnify the political power of elderly Americans. Another pertinent fact is that older people are more likely than younger citizens to vote. In fact, we Americans vote in a ratio roughly equivalent to our age: about 20 percent at age twenty, 30 percent at age thirty, 40 percent at age forty, 50 percent at age fifty, and about 60 percent at age sixty. This accentuates the political power of the thirty-five million of us over sixty-five years old (just three million in 1900), who will remain politically alert during our average of nineteen more years of life.

As inevitable changes are made in laws governing Social Security, Medicare, and Medicaid, we must be vigilant and forceful in protecting those among us who are most vulnerable and in need of financial assistance.

With all these advantages, it shouldn't be too surprising that the elderly are relatively self-sufficient. Contrary to general belief, only 5 percent of us live in nursing homes (a number that is decreasing), while just 15 percent receive any financial help from their families.

5

Family Accommodations We Have Made

It's nicer now that our children have reached our age.
—*NEW YORKER* CARTOON

The cohesive families of three or more generations that we knew in our youth now dissolve when the youngest children go off to college or to work in distant places—often when the parents are forty to forty-five years old. As a result, there is a general division of modern American families into two nuclear groups: (1) young adults with their children, and (2) their older parents. This distinction is especially pronounced if the two families are separated geographically, which is often the case.

This change has affected the status of many of us

older people, as our parenting responsibilities end much earlier and more permanently than before. Also, a few decades ago wisdom and knowledge were transmitted orally, from dominant parents and teachers to the younger members of their families or communities. Telephones, radios, television, and the Internet have short-circuited these old customs, putting a premium on youthful and innovative ideas and making the old-fashioned prudence of seniors something to be ignored, pitied, or even ridiculed. Nowadays we struggle to stay abreast of the transient and ever more radical customs, language, and music of our children and grandchildren.

At the same time, the shift from farms to urban life has decreased our usefulness as workers, and there has been a significant weakening of mutual responsibility within families, brought about mostly by Social Security and Medicare.

As with most other couples, profound changes have taken place between Rosalynn and me, and as we've moved into our retirement years we've had

to continue reconciling our inherent personal differences. It has not always been easy. Rosalynn's
family background and mine are dramatically different. When we left the navy and moved back to our
hometown of Plains, I was amazed at her family's
habits. Her relatives would have family reunions
each year, where 100 to 150 people met on a particular Sunday. They would bring and consume deli-
cious prize recipes, meet the new in-laws, exclaim
over the uniqueness of babies, reminisce about former times, give a one-dollar prize for the oldest, the
youngest, and the one who traveled the farthest, and
then all go home to await another year's assembly.

None of my parents' relatives ever dreamed of
having a family gathering of any kind, and perhaps
for good reason. My great-grandfather and my grandfather were both killed in violent arguments. And
although my father's generation seemed at least to
have peaceful relationships, I never knew his first
cousins, who lived within ten miles of our home.

One of the most surprising discoveries when I
began dating Rosalynn was that meals at her home
were so relaxed and totally uneventful. Folks around
the table could spend a couple of hours talking about
relatively insignificant events within their family,
among their friends, at the schoolhouse, or in the
Plains community. I don't remember a cross word

ever being spoken. This was completely different from meals at our house. My mother's rule was that she or any of us children could read at the table, so our conversations were often limited. Any discussions, of necessity, had to be more interesting than what we were reading, and were usually brief, narrowly focused, and often involved controversial subjects. Any assembly of Carters was almost always an adventure, and it was only the controlling influence of my father that preserved peace in our family.

I was dominant when we were a young married couple and as our young children were growing up, and we adopted the habits of the Carters. We read at the table, our discussions were often intense and usually restricted to "important" subjects, and we rarely reached out to other members of our family.

This has changed. The sharper differences have faded during the fifty-two years that Rosalynn and I have spent together. Of necessity, we each had to accommodate the preferences of the other, and our challenge has been to extract the best from both families. This evolutionary trend was accelerated when I was no longer president and we were more on equal terms in every aspect of life.

My habits and interests are still different from Rosalynn's, but at first there was a greater chasm between us. In the navy I was constantly traveling and expanding my familiarity with the outside world. I had grown up enjoying outdoor activities such as hunting, fishing, camping, tennis, hiking, and running. During the last fifty years, sometimes at first reluctantly, Rosalynn has agreed to join me in many of these things. She has become a good tennis player and an excellent fly fisher; we run together several times a week, and climb the same mountains; her involvement in business, politics, and global activities equals mine. When I began writing this paragraph, I went into the other room to ask Rosalynn what early preferences she had that I have adopted. We couldn't think of any, except that I have accepted with increasing fervor her early preference to stay at home, to be with each other and with our children, and to reach out to other members of our family. On balance, I may have learned more than I taught her.

Since she first began helping keep books at Carter's Warehouse, Rosalynn has been a full partner in everything we have done. However, each of us has our own responsibilities and circle of friends. Although we make most of our foreign trips together, mostly to Africa, Latin America, or Asia, we tend to divide many of the duties of The Carter Center. Work with the elderly and with mental health are under Rosalynn's direction, and I participate only when asked. She is with me, taking careful notes, when I am attempting to negotiate a peace agreement between disputing factions, and is a full participant when we monitor elections in newly emerging democracies. But she manages to avoid most of the fund-raising excursions and the more tedious discussions with American or foreign officials. We also go our separate ways as professors at Emory University or when we lecture at other colleges.

I compute the relatively complicated settlements involving our farms. Before we slowly acquired most of their shares, I had to account to as many as a dozen co-owners of the property originally owned by my father and his siblings. Including the various crops, dealings with government agencies, handling the sale of timber products, and negotiating with active farmers who rent our cultivated lands, this is a significant task. But it fades into relative insignificance when compared to Rosalynn's accounting and financial responsibilities. She still keeps all the books for our family, pays bills, balances bank accounts, communicates with our stockbroker, and maintains some complicated financial arrangements with our children and grandchildren. Even in these duties, we prefer to do our own thing. She has always rejected any offers I have made to assist her when I noticed that she was irritable or distressed, had to work late at night, or seemed to be behind in her work. I feel the same way in not wanting her involved in the detailed farm partnerships.

We are still close, after fifty-two years together.

Driving on the interstate highway in Atlanta to go to The Carter Center, for several months we regularly passed a large billboard advertising country music. The sign said, "My wife ran off with my best friend, and I miss him." This doesn't apply to us. We seem to be bound together with ever-increasing bonds as we've grown older and need each other more. When we are apart for just a day or so, I have the same hollow feeling of loneliness and unassuaged desire as when I was away at sea for a week or more during the first years of our marriage.

There is no doubt that we now cherish each day more than when we were younger. Our primary purpose in our golden years is not just to stay alive as long as we can, but to savor every opportunity for pleasure, excitement, adventure, and fulfillment.

After all our children became young adults and moved away, we were faced with the inevitability of living in the same house alone. We quickly learned that we had to give each other some space—an almost inviolate separation unless both of us wish to be together. It's the same house that we built in 1961, except that I established my workplace and library in what was originally our garage, and she converted one of our boys' rooms into her own office. In between is a kitchen and den, which are considered to be neutral ground. We have a seldom-used intercom system, and we keep our doors shut when concentrating deeply on writing or other tasks. I like classical (or sometimes country) music while I work, and Rosalynn prefers total silence. There are regular times during the day when we get together, for meals or late in the afternoon when we exercise or perhaps catch a mess of fish in one of our ponds and then cook supper together.

We have learned over time that there are a few significant disagreements that are best not explored too thoroughly. Some of these differences involve relationships with our four children and their families. They are all highly individualistic and we have to deal with them in different ways, so Rosalynn and I naturally divide this responsibility.

There were times in our lives when a dispute lasted several weeks, causing both of us great but often unadmitted distress. We still have our share of disagreements and even vehement arguments, but we've finally become mature enough not to dwell on them nearly as long. After a relatively brief cooling-off period, we either ignore the differences or confront each other frankly and try to discuss them rationally.

One day a few years ago, when we were more angry with each other than usual, I decided to go one step further. In my woodshop I prepared a thin sheet of walnut about the size of a small bank check and carved on it, "Each evening, forever, this is good for an apology—or forgiveness—as you desire." I signed it and gave it to Rosalynn. Although it has sometimes been difficult, so far I have been able to honor my promise.

As we've grown older, Rosalynn and I have had to analyze our mutual talents, experiences from earlier years, mandatory and voluntary obligations to our family, the degree of our involvement with others, our financial status, and what we want to be our legacy. We've had to accept the earlier decisions we made and the consequences of them, and to realize that there will not be many more major forks in our lives' roads where we can make choices.

Our questions have been the same as those of many other couples. Did we have long-standing desires or ambitions that we could now fulfill? Were there old acquaintances we might want to renew, or estrangements from other people to be resolved? Which of our worries or concerns could be ignored, either because they were not really important or because we couldn't do anything about them? After having observed a number of deaths of our loved ones, what lessons had we learned that might apply to ourselves as we faced our later years and inevitable death? Could we discuss these sensitive questions between ourselves and perhaps with our children, and exhibit sound judgment or wisdom in making the necessary decisions? How many responsibilities could we accept ourselves, and what help would we need? What had been our total accumulation of possessions, and what did we want to do with what we had?

When we finally decided to face these issues together, we weren't even sure of our insurance coverage, the exact property holdings, the terms of our wills, or how we wanted to be treated during the final days of our lives. In a somewhat methodical way over the last few years, we have answered most of the questions and now are much more knowledgeable about the ones we still have to face.

The few that relate to our own children have been most difficult. As we've struggled to deal with our immediate family as a group of fellow adults, I have had to acknowledge some of the mistakes I've made, if only in order to correct them. It wasn't until I bared my inner thoughts in poetry that I was able to face the complicated relationship I had with my father—and to realize how similar my attitude was toward my own sons.

I WANTED TO SHARE MY FATHER'S WORLD

This is a pain I mostly hide,
but ties of blood, or seed, endure,
and even now I feel inside
the hunger for his outstretched hand,

a man's embrace to take me in,
the need for just a word of praise.

I despised the discipline
he used to shape what I should be,
now owning up that he might feel
his own pain when he punished me.

I didn't show my need to him,
since his response to an appeal
would not have meant as much to me,
or been as real.

From those rare times when we did cross
the bridge between us, the pure joy
survives.

      I never put aside
the past resentments of the boy
until, with my own sons, I shared
his final hours, and came to see
what he'd become, or always was—
the father who will never cease to be
alive in me.

We've come to realize that our children are now mature, basically established in life, set in their ways, and not very dependent on us to care for their needs, except in emergencies. Instead of being powerful and dominant, I have had to accept the fact that other members of our family have become much more independent and less subject to my influence or direction. With the previous deference to us as dominant parents no longer there, we have had to back away and assess how we could retain a modicum of respect and attractiveness.

At the same time we are experiencing an indescribable blessing of aging: grandchildren. Now ranging in age from kindergarteners to recent college graduates, our sons' children comprise an intriguing and diverse group with whom we have become increasingly interrelated. The occasional tensions that existed with some of our children don't apply to them, and the degree of our voluntary responsibilities toward them is something we decide. Consulting with their parents, we are able to assess their varying needs and have enjoyed devising approaches that let us relate in a constructive and harmonious way, without coming between them and their parents. Also, even more than our children, they seem to represent our inclination toward a lasting legacy.

But like other expanding families, ours has had a tendency to separate and perhaps fragment. Rosalynn and I have had to face this situation at various times in recent years, with Amy off at college in Rhode Island, Tennessee, and Louisiana and our oldest son living near Chicago, then in Cleveland, and later in Bermuda. For a while we managed to see them all several times a year, at least for Thanksgiving and Christmas. However, we were increasingly in competition with in-laws even for these two special days, and had to resort to another ploy.

Since Rosalynn and I travel so much during the year, we accumulate significant frequent flyer mileage. Each year we have used this and some of our savings to take our entire family on a trip between Christmas and New Year's, when our grandchildren are out of school. We usually have a round-robin discussion among the family members until a consensus is reached on our next destination, and then make the often complicated arrangements. We have been fishing along the east coast of Florida and the west coast of Mexico, camping in the jungles of Belize, sightseeing in the Florida Keys, swimming and diving on Contadora Island in Panama, skiing in Colorado, following the young ones through Disney World, and sailing on several Caribbean cruises.

There are now more than twenty of us, and some of the trips are quite expensive, but we consider these excursions to be among our best bargains. They let us get to know each other, offer enough flexibility to provide pleasure to all age groups, encourage more frequent visits during the rest of the year, and also give us a rare chance to discuss family financial affairs and long-range plans with our children and older grandchildren.

Earlier in our marriage, when the cost of family vacations was a paramount consideration, we found great opportunities renting a few less expensive houses during the off-season in resort areas or in nearby state parks. Nowadays, we can let our children share as much of the cost as they can afford.

6

Planning for Retirement Years

*Anybody who can still do at sixty what he was
doing at twenty wasn't doing much at twenty.*

There are two periods in our lives when we have
exceptional freedom: at college age and when we
begin our retirement years. At those times we have
relatively few restrictions and obligations, a clear
concept of our fairly unalterable financial status,
and minimal limits on what and how many things
we can do. It's obviously best to begin planning
early, but it's too much to expect young college students to realize that their curriculum should prepare
them for an entire life and not just for a profession
before retirement. It seems obvious to me that a

broad liberal arts background is valuable all the way through our final years, but our adult experiences invariably add additional dimensions to whatever early education we had.

College can require hard and sustained work in the classroom, so retirees have an even greater degree of freedom. Each day offers us twenty-four hours to be used and enjoyed, but this degree of flexibility means that careful and thoughtful decisions are really beneficial. We try to make careful plans for everything else, so why not our later years? We can expect to spend about half our adult lives in retirement, but many of us don't prepare properly, except for trying to accumulate a financial base large enough to support ourselves. Based on my own experience, I can understand the reluctance to make such decisions—or at least the desire to postpone them. Nonetheless, such decisions should be made.

Productive planning requires some self-assessment, and we'll likely face an element of rigidity—a reluctance or inability to change, even with age. If, as a young person, we are timid or outgoing, selfish or generous, retiring or ambitious, cowardly or courageous, we are likely to be the same way as an elderly person. Although we can certainly change some attitudes during our lives, our early self-destructive habits are also likely to persist, including smoking, poor food choices, excessive drinking, and lack of exercise. In most cases, of course, these may protect us from old age altogether!

At some time—not too late, one hopes—all of us need to prepare more specifically for the later days. Crafting a piece of furniture, writing a poem or a book, painting a picture, laying out a vacation route, or just rearranging the furniture are all processes similar to planning a retirement life. We have to assess our potential and limits, envision the final result that we desire, make ambitious plans accordingly, and then implement them. It is encouraging to realize that we older people can now build on an entire previous life of education, training, and experience.

With more time on our hands, the least we can do is to select a few things that we really like that might still be enjoyed when we're eighty years old. One approach is simply to enumerate the times and places in our lives that have been most delightful, and then repeat them. Some of these may have been the environment of a remote place on an expensive foreign vacation, but chances are that we can also remember some relaxing activities near home that cost little or nothing.

In addition to transient pleasures, it's also helpful to recapitulate our personal accomplishments or interests of the past, regardless of what they were. These would go far beyond our previous professions, and might include music, art, poetry, botany, reading, dancing, travel, history, gardening, writing, or family genealogy. It is likely that we were frustrated in pursuing some of these interests during our younger years because we had to devote most of our time to earning a living and caring for our family. We can now make time to resurrect one or more of these subjects, learn more about them, and develop a new hobby or even a profession.

The choices are almost unlimited. We have a friend near our mountain cabin who was a Delta Airlines pilot until he reached mandatory retirement age. By then he had built a shop, bought a large machine lathe, and completed courses at a nearby vocational school so that he could become expert in its use. I've enjoyed woodworking and writing, and expect to take up painting again sometime in the future.

We should consider our life as expanding, not contracting, and modern technology can help to make this ambition easier to realize. A person my age now has the remaining potential that only a much younger person had just a few decades ago. We not only have longer to live, but in some ways each year now equals several years in olden times. We are exposed to fifteen times as much knowledge as Aristotle was; many of us travel as much in a year as Marco Polo did in a lifetime. In effect, as far as knowledge and observations are concerned, our life experiences encompass the equivalent of a thousand years in older generations. Our number of years has increased by 50 percent, but our functional years have grown by 1,000 percent. (This does not mean necessarily that we have more wisdom or retain more useful knowledge.)

Beginning in my late fifties, my own life has been greatly affected by computers. Every day that I am at home I use word processing software for writing books, newspaper and magazine articles, poems, letters, and my diary. Even when I'm traveling I stay in touch with Rosalynn, my children and grandchildren, my office, and friends by E-mail. In fact, I correspond much more now with all of them than I did when letters had to be written and mailed. Since Plains is relatively isolated and we don't get a major newspaper the day it's published, I review the electronic editions of the *New York Times* and other news media early each morning. I also search the Internet for other information as I need it.

Despite this, none of us can afford to let ourselves become societal dependents, seduced into dormancy or inactivity by the same technology that offers expanded access to knowledge. As anyone who visits a nursing home could deduce, the average older person now watches television forty-three hours each week. There is a great world away from a soft chair and a flickering screen. There's no need for most of us to be so passive. We can still explore some of the more active pleasures of the "good old days."

7

Good Health
for the Elderly

Getting a second doctor's opinion is
kinda like switching slot machines.

Since we reached retirement age, Rosalynn and I
have found ourselves immersed in confusing and
often conflicting advice on what we can do to stay
healthy. We are overwhelmed with books, maga-
zines, news articles, and particularly advertisements
that bombard the consciousness of senior citizens
who are concerned about good health and have
some money to spend on the advertised products.

It is interesting how certain television broadcasts
target us. The most obvious example is the noon or
evening news, which hardly ever includes commer-

cials that would appeal to young people. Instead, it is filled with ads for incontinence pads, remedies for constipation, denture adhesives, vitamin-charged drinks that give pep to the aged, and medicines that control heartburn and prevent osteoporosis.

Perhaps because of the confusion, studies show that very few elderly people make a real effort to maintain a program of proper diet and exercise. Rosalynn and I find this to be a somewhat enjoyable challenge.

We have learned that it is *not* true that we face an inevitable decline in our health as we grow older. Moderate exercise can have dramatic results in maintaining our lung capacity, bone strength, and mental sharpness. Along with prescribed medicines, exercise also helps to lower blood pressure, cholesterol, body fat, and blood sugar.

When we are traveling long distances and spending many hours in meetings, we jog (or walk) a few miles very early in the mornings when there is not much traffic and the smog is at a minimum. If we can't run on the streets, we find a nearby park. At home we usually exercise late in the afternoon, jogging, playing tennis, riding bikes, or taking long walks in our woodlands.

Rosalynn is an excellent cook and has long been fascinated with proper nutrition and how to apply some simple but important rules to our daily meals. She has been able to accommodate our lifetime preference for southern farm foods and cook them so that they meet modern health standards. She is a painstaking shopper, examining labels to minimize cholesterol, calories, salt, and saturated fats. During an average day we have about eight moderate servings of bread or cereal, three to five servings of vegetables and fruit, and a couple servings of meat and low-fat dairy products. We do eat desserts, almost always low-fat ice cream, frozen yogurt, Jell-O, cookies, and the like.

One thing that requires the most self-discipline is weighing myself every morning. Sometimes I hate to look at the scale, because if I'm over my desired weight, I have to force myself to cut back that day on calories or take a little extra exercise.

What is good health? It's not just the absence of a physical illness or something like a long vacation without pain. I would say that good health, more than being able-bodied, involves self-regard, control over our own affairs, strong ties with other people, and a purpose in life. These things don't just evolve automatically, but have to be sought and maintained.

Many of us are afflicted with bad health, or at least the fear of a serious illness or premature death. What are the causes of our suffering or discomfort? In order to get scientifically accurate information on this subject, The Carter Center sponsored a definitive conference called Closing the Gap, attended by 120 of America's foremost experts on health, including several Nobel laureates. It became obvious that we have much more of a role to play in our health and longevity than do hospitals, medicines, and high technology. Two thirds of our physical ailments and premature deaths are caused by our own deliberate choice of lifestyle and can be delayed or prevented with proper habits.

Here is a brief summary of these experts' simple but profound advice:

1. Do not smoke.
2. Maintain recommended body weight.
3. Exercise regularly.
4. Minimize consumption of foods high in cholesterol and saturated fats, sugar, and salt.
5. Do not drink excessively, and never drive when drinking.
6. Fasten seat belts.

7. Remove handguns from the home.
8. Have regular medical checkups, including blood-pressure tests.

These are all obvious, but nationwide studies show that a very small portion of senior citizens observe them. This neglect costs Americans about a third of our useful lives. To be more specific, a recent issue of the *Journal of the American Medical Association* reported that the number one cause of death in America is tobacco, which causes more than four hundred thousand fatalities a year. In fact, thirty-five-year-olds who smoke cigarettes have already reduced their life expectancy by more than fifteen years! The second cause of premature death is improper diet, with three hundred thousand deaths each year, and the third is alcohol, with a hundred thousand, including accidents caused by drunken driving.

The conclusions and recommendations of our conference are still applicable, but of course the final advice should come from a trusted family doctor who is personally familiar with individual circumstances. Obviously, at our age an annual physical examination is mandatory. If we fear having heart disease, Alzheimer's, a broken hip, a stroke, diabetes, or cancer, it is obvious that we must have regular physical checkups. How else can we know the threat of these crippling or fatal diseases and act early enough to treat or prevent them? Great strides have been made in reducing the threat of all of them. Such simple things as a daily aspirin or a calcium supplement can be very beneficial. There are dozens of drugs now being developed by major pharmaceutical companies to enhance our quality of life—or at least to delay the consequences of aging. The most famous of all is Viagra, designed to improve the sex life of impotent men, but many others can help to correct sleep difficulties, prevent osteoporosis, control incontinence, increase energy levels, lower cholesterol levels, and even improve memory.

A serious warning should be included here: We shouldn't take too many different kinds of medicine. Some older people are excessively concerned about their health, like to tell others about their ailments, or just enjoy visiting different doctors' offices. In the process, they often accumulate multiple suggestions or prescriptions and find themselves with an unnecessary and confusing accumulation of drugs that they feel obligated to take. A few years ago Rosalynn noticed that her mother, then almost ninety years old, was trying to remember which of almost two dozen medicines was the next one she was supposed to take. A competent physician examined both her and her array of drugs, discovered that most were useless and some even counterproductive, and greatly simplified her medication.

One remaining problem, however, is that many physicians look only at a current health problem or limit their routine examinations to weight, blood pressure, cholesterol levels, heart rate, balance, and a few questions about physical abilities. They rarely question the patient about personal habits that might cause even more serious ailments. After our Closing the Gap conference, we developed what we called a Health Risk Appraisal (HRA), a self-administered test that explores a person's personal habits, including smoking, drinking, exercise, diet, and the observance of normal safety precautions. The results predict how many more years of life we can expect compared to an average American of the same age if we maintain our present lifestyle. It also estimates how much longer we could live if we adopt—or give up—certain habits.

There is still a difference between how long we

live and how much we enjoy living. With reasonably good health, there are two crucial factors in how happy or successful an older person is: (1) *having a purpose in life* and (2) *maintaining quality relationships with others.* So other HRA inquiries might well be added, such as "Are you doing any interesting things?" "What goals are you trying to accomplish?" "Do you think you can achieve them?" "What are the best relationships you have with other people?" "Are you of help to one another?" "How do you spend most of your time?"

This kind of self-examination is also the best preparation for a successful transition from a job to retirement. I've known all too many friends down through the years who worked hard all their lives, accumulating wealth. Then they made some last-minute and regretful or halfhearted plans for retirement and died within a few weeks or months after leaving their jobs. Tragically, they didn't derive much pleasure from the long and dreary process of making more money, and they never had a chance to enjoy the things for which they spent a lifetime saving.

A recent major study of more than forty thousand older people showed that some physical exercise is the most important single thing that we can do to stay healthy. Just gardening or walking for thirty minutes a day is almost as beneficial as exercise that is much more vigorous. The study found that with exercise, many people in their nineties were able to double their endurance and make great improvements in their *mental* well-being! Unfortunately, the same study revealed that about half of those over seventy-five are "couch potatoes," and only a fifth exercise regularly.

One of the most remarkable discoveries in recent years is that our self-esteem can materially affect our physical health. Apparently, in some cases this even includes the remission of cancer. In one definitive test, confidence and ease of mind brought about by religious beliefs, daily meditation, and group therapy sessions resulted in more than two additional years of life compared to a control group with the same illnesses but without such reassurances. Medical scientists believe that such experiences result in a sense of purpose in life, self-regard, and emotional bonds with others. We need to feel that we can create the circumstances for a good life, not just give up hope and become inactive and often withdrawn.

The key point is that physical and mental activities strengthen each other and provide the necessary foundation for successful aging. The bottom line is to take on almost *any* tasks that are interesting and challenging—the more the better. We all know from experience that talking, touching, and relating to other people are necessary for our development and happiness, from infancy through all other stages of life. As we get older it is important to avoid mental dormancy and to keep our minds occupied. This doesn't need to be anything special, but can include such simple things as conversations with others in person or by telephone, reading, correspondence with friends, crossword puzzles, games, hobbies, or planning a garden.

Some of the most valuable advice I've ever re-ceived is that it's better to use recreation to preserve health rather than to use medicines and treatment to *regain* health. This is true both for mental and physical well-being. A diverse life—filled with changes, experiments, different kinds of repose, in-novations, and adventures—is one that is much less likely to be afflicted with illness. This means that a few dollars or days spent pursuing a hobby or pastime is a sound investment, paying off in both enjoyment and in avoided medical expenses.

If we are not fortunate enough to have good health, it is a sign of maturity to accept our physical limitations, the prospect of some disabilities, and the increasing imminence of death. Those who are hard of hearing should not hesitate to get a hearing aid; it's no different from using eyeglasses when our sight is not perfect. If we have difficulty moving about or maintaining our balance, we must not be embarrassed about using a cane, walker, or even a wheelchair. All of these are better than being embarrassed, withdrawn, or immobile with a false sense of self-pride. Even with partial disability, we should continue to grow, try new things, explore interests of our early lives, and take advantage of nearby universities and libraries as well as modern technology. In fact, there are Internet forums that deal with opportunities for older people, one of which is at www.seniornet.org/solutions.

A partnership with others will often give us the extra strength or encouragement to pursue good health habits successfully. What kinds of support are most valuable among older people? At age sixty-five, people can expect to be dependent on others during about 15 percent of their remaining time, and by eighty-five they will require some assistance during about half of the remaining years. It is obvious that, as much as possible, there should be mutual assistance among elders who live together. Chores like cooking, shopping, cleaning, and the administration of medicines can be divided somewhat equally or assumed by whoever is best able to perform them at a particular time. The other kind of support—emotional—is known to be even more crucial for a successful life. This relationship involves the sharing of thoughts and experiences through a partner's friendly presence, a demonstration of concern, normal conversation, and shared recreation. An interesting statistic is that the average older person has about ten personal acquaintances, including family, neighbors, friends, fellow church members, and so on. It doesn't take much effort to strengthen these ties or to expand the circle.

A cautionary comment is necessary here, in response to the single most serious concern of older people: the fear of being dependent on others. Of the 95 percent of people over sixty-five who do not live in nursing homes, fewer than 5 percent say they now need help with their physical needs. Even when we become feeble in some ways, it is better to be as independent as possible, resisting the temptation to rely on others to do things we are able to do ourselves. It is dangerous to sink into inactivity by accepting help or services that we can provide for ourselves. The best intentions of others can change us into television-watching vegetables.

8

Seventy,
Going on Eighty

When you're pushing seventy,
that's exercise enough.

This chapter will be about how Rosalynn and I have evolved customs and habits that shape our lives together in our seventies. I realize that we might have a fuller and more active life than some readers. If so, it's because we have had such varied experiences and have so far been blessed with good health. The delineation of our recreational activities is not designed to be competitive with others, but just to show that people of our age have good ideas to share with each other. One of the most delightful and exciting developments in my relationship with

Rosalynn has been our agreement to learn new things together. Perhaps our experiences are typical or at least suggest some similar thoughts among readers.

FISHING

Since childhood, I had fished for bass and bream in the warm South Georgia waters. As governor, I began fishing for trout in the cold waters of the Chattahoochee River. Later, during our presidential years, Rosalynn tried a few casts at Yellowstone National Park; then we invited some of the most famous and accomplished fly-fishing teachers and writers to join us for a weekend at Camp David. Since then, both of us have steadily increased our fly-fishing skills. Now my casts are somewhat longer, but hers are more precise at shorter distances. We have found opportunities to fish in Alaska, New Zealand, Finland, Canada, England, Ireland, Wales, Japan, Switzerland, and Chile, and our children and grandchildren have joined us on some of the finest streams of America. This hobby, or art, has added a wonderful new dimension to our lives. Like golf or chess, fly fishing offers a never-ending challenge to improve skills, practice, and knowledge. One of my greatest pleasures has been to teach my twelve-year-old grandson to tie flies for himself and for us.

MOUNTAIN CLIMBING

When I was sixty years old we decided to go trekking in the Himalayas, and we became acquainted with the beauties of Nepal and the extraordinary character of the Sherpa guides who accompanied us. We climbed quite rapidly, and although some of our party had to return to Katmandu because of altitude sickness, Rosalynn accompanied me to an altitude above three miles, and I climbed on to about 1,100 feet above the Everest base camp. This whetted our appetite, and four years later we climbed Mount Kilimanjaro. Rosalynn and our three oldest grandchildren made it to 17,500 feet before returning to a lower level, but my sons and I made it up to the crater. We arrived at the top at sunrise, in a blinding snowstorm, just a couple of degrees from the equator! Our most difficult climb, perhaps because of advancing age, was when I was seventy and we made a one-day trek up and down Japan's Mount Fuji.

BIRD-WATCHING

After climbing Kilimanjaro, we visited a few of the game preserves in Tanzania. We started a contest between adults and children: Who could see the first of a new species of animal? We saw many elephants, lions, water buffaloes, giraffes, hyenas, various kinds of monkeys, and ostriches. Expanding our rules to include small birds, we were soon in a new and even more exciting phase of competition. Fortunately for us, our driver had studied ornithology in college and could identify the birds we saw. Within three days we had sighted 126 different ones, and Rosalynn and I had become lifetime bird-watchers. Since then, we try to find an expert in each new country we visit, and we spend several early-morning hours expanding our list in city parks, along seashores, or in jungle areas. At home, we participate in the annual breeder bird survey within a few miles of Plains. Bird-watching has added another dimension to our lives.

SKIING

One of our most interesting and challenging experiences was the result of an early annual family outing. We had a friend from White House years who lived in New Mexico and made arrangements for us to spend a week at a ski resort in Taos. We looked at some of the brochures and noticed that these were some of the steepest and most challenging slopes in the Rockies. Before leaving home, Rosalynn and I decided that we would let our children and grand-children take advantage of the new sport, while we would get some rest around the fireplaces of the ski lodge and perhaps enjoy snowmobiling. After all, I was sixty-two years old, and Rosalynn was just three years younger.

Needless to say, however, at the resort we re-sponded to the pleas and taunts of the younger Carters and were soon with them on the learners' slopes. At the end of three days we were on top of the mountain and descending carefully with our skis in a rigid wedge. Since then we have enjoyed the Rocky Mountain resorts every year and seen even our smallest grandchildren whizzing past us with abandon. This has added another nice dimension to our lives.

TENNIS

I had played tennis most of my life, beginning as a child with my father. But it was only after Rosa-lynn decided to learn the sport that we built a tennis court behind our house. Since then she has had a few lessons, spent hours with a ball-throwing machine, and has improved steadily so as to be quite competitive with me. I have never deliberately let her win a point, but I give her some advantages. She has use of the doubles court on my end, and a beginning point when I am ahead of her in games. Although I still have an advantage in serving, she is now equal to me in ground strokes, and each of our matches is a hard-fought contest with the outcome usually in doubt.

WRITING BOOKS

Another quite different adventure on which we have embarked is writing books. I wrote my first one in 1975, something of an autobiography and an explanation of my political philosophy as I began my presidential campaign. Later, after I was victorious in Iowa, New Hampshire, and Florida, the book became a best-seller, and a million copies were rushed into print. Since then, I have written eleven other books, including a presidential memoir, histories, an outdoor journal, a collection of my poems, and an account of my experiences in mediating disputes. Rosalynn's autobiography was number one on the

New York Times best-seller list. She has since written one on caregiving, and her third book, on mental health, has just been published. I'm working on a novel set in the South during the later years of the Revolutionary War. We now edit each other's work but will never write one again as coauthors, after an earlier effort almost broke up our marriage. Except for this trying experience, our writing has drawn us together. We share the responsibilities of negotiating advances, meeting deadlines, working with editors, and going on book tours after our work arrives in bookstores.

CABINETMAKING

I developed an interest in cabinetmaking as a Future Farmer of America in high school, and I was able to build some much-needed furniture in navy hobby shops when Rosalynn and I first set up housekeeping. Later, I didn't have the time or the place to develop this as a hobby. When I left the White House, my staff and cabinet members took up a collection and gave me a superb going-away present: a complete set of woodworking tools. Since then I have studied books and attended weekend schools to learn more advanced techniques of joinery and finishing, and I have designed and crafted perhaps a hundred pieces of furniture.

I'm a morning person, and when doing office work or writing, I get up very early and put in two or three hours of my most productive work before breakfast time. Then I go back to the computer until my mind begins to wander and my back gets sore. Since my woodshop is only a few steps from my home office, going there has been a perfect vacation—like another world—and also something of a private place. When I am sketching a piece of furniture, selecting the appropriate wood from my stock, and then fashioning it into a chair, table, chest, bed, or cabinet, I become totally absorbed in the work, and time passes like magic.

We have tried a few things that were more than we could handle or that we decided to abandon as a partnership. For instance, during our canoeing days on the Chattahoochee and Chatooga Rivers, we also took up kayaking. We learned to roll one in a swimming pool, but decided that the vagaries of river currents and rocky bottoms were too much for us.

HUNTING

Hunting is one sport that Rosalynn is reluctant to share. Beginning as a farm boy, I have been a proud owner and trainer of bird dogs and adept in the use of guns. After returning home from the navy, I had two good dogs, and finally induced Rosalynn to accompany me to an area of our farm where there was a good crop of bobwhite quail. I taught her all the safety precautions, how to load one of my single-trigger double-barrel shotguns, and we stepped away from our pickup truck into a field of broom sedge and blackberry briars. Almost immediately a covey of quail flushed. I shouted, "Shoot, shoot"; she pushed the safety forward, aimed, and nervously pulled the trigger. To her surprise, both barrels went off sequentially, and she has refused to shoot again except at fixed targets under carefully controlled conditions. She still likes to walk with me and watch the dogs work, however.

I don't hunt as much as I used to, but still try to harvest two wild turkeys each season for our family's Thanksgiving and Christmas feasts. Although she doesn't shoot, Rosalynn often goes with me into the forests before daylight, finds a concealed spot near me, surrounds herself with a small camouflaged blind, and enjoys the ambience of the awakening wilderness. Completely hidden and quiet as we listen for gobblers, we are approached within a few feet by songbirds, deer, raccoons, opossums, pileated woodpeckers, and even coyotes and armadillos, relative newcomers to our area. These excursions in the early spring let us examine our woodlands closely and plan for the year's timber management, thinning, cutting, and replanting.

Rosalynn and I are almost as active now as we have ever been, writing, teaching, caring for our farmland and personal finances, and serving at The Carter Center, with its multiple projects all over the world. As difficult as it will be, it is time for us to decide how to set more stringent priorities, retaining some responsibilities that will be commensurate with our abilities and relinquishing others that can be assumed by younger people. We have already had to face the fact that we are not as irreplaceable as we once were, and we're trying to evolve wise decisions about reducing our active involvement while retaining some means of observing or perhaps monitoring some of the issues in which we have a deep and abiding interest.

Also, although we try to take care of ourselves, both of us have been to the hospital several times for brief treatment during the last few years. This is a reminder that we face some inevitable changes in our health as we grow older.

I haven't yet given up any of the active sports of my earlier years, although I have had to cut back on some of them. Now I run three miles a day with Rosalynn instead of the seven miles I ran while president, and we limit our tennis to two sets of about twenty games. Our bike rides are usually ten to fifteen miles over country roads, often to and from our farm. We wade more carefully and are probably retaining our fly-fishing skills, but there is little doubt that my shooting eye is not as sharp.

With weaker knees and bones that are more brittle, I've abandoned the black-diamond ski slopes and moguls. In softball, my pitch is as accurate as ever, but there is little power in my drives, and my baserunning is much slower and more cautious. Last summer I pitched seven innings a game for my softball team in Plains, but I'm kept from being too proud by reading about other older athletes. A recent front-page article in the *New York Times* described a softball league in Sun City, Florida, where the pitcher was eighty and had to take eleven pills a day to control his arthritis. Recently they forced the retirement of one of their ninety-year-old teammates because the ball, which he could no longer see, frequently hit him. He took up lawn bowling. Their left fielder was eighty-three, and the youngest player was sixty-nine. There were frequent dropped balls, bruises, and sore muscles, but the men could hardly wait each year for the next season to begin.

Recently I talked to John Kelley, who was born in 1907, finished fifty-eight Boston Marathons, and ran his sixtieth Boston Marathon at eighty-three. He won in 1935 and 1945 and has been runner-up seven times. Kelley competed in the Olympics in Berlin (1936) and London (1940). He was grand marshal of the Boston Marathon in 1995 and 1997, and is very proud of a statue of him on "Heartbreak Hill," the most difficult stretch on the marathon course. Twice a widower, he described his new love affair and told me that he still jogs every day, swims, and takes long walks with his new sweetheart.

When I was married at the age of twenty-two and relishing an active sex life, I assumed that this was a pleasure that my middle-aged parents rarely, if ever, enjoyed. Now, well past seventy, Rosalynn and I have learned to accommodate each other's desires more accurately and generously, and have never had a more complete and enjoyable relationship.

Studies at Duke University confirm what we have experienced: Many men and women maintain sexual interest and activity as they grow older, even throughout their seventies. Masters and Johnson's research revealed that eighty-year-old men are perfectly capable of experiencing orgasm and can have frequent and enjoyable erections. In fact, a healthy man who has self-confidence and an accommodating mate can enjoy satisfying and imaginative love play throughout life.

There is another fact that is quite sobering, however: About 10 percent of people with AIDS are senior citizens, many of whom never considered the need for practicing safe sex at their advanced age. In fact, medical specialists say that women past menopause are, for some reason, particularly vulnerable to HIV infection.

In an unfortunate interview with *Playboy* magazine during my presidential campaign in 1976, I quoted a verse from Jesus' Sermon on the Mount and admitted that I had been guilty of feeling lust for other women before I married Rosalynn. This created a wave of publicity, and I dropped fifteen points in public approval and almost lost the election. In 1995 I was signing my volume of poetry in a bookstore near Harvard University. There was a long line, and I was trying to sign the books as rapidly as possible and still make eye contact and exchange a few polite words with each customer. One attractive woman, perhaps in her late thirties, said, "Mr. President, I remember that interview you had with *Playboy* magazine." Everyone got quiet, and then she added, "If you still have lust in your heart, I'm available." I blushed beet red while the crowd roared with laughter. I have to admit that, at my age, it's an encounter I remember with pleasure.

9

Facing the
End

There aren't many of the good old days left.

With advancing age, all of us witness with increasing despair the deaths of our friends and contemporaries. Obligations to attend funerals become more frequent, and we are faced with personal proof of life expectancy statistics. In June 1996 I attended the fiftieth anniversary of my class at the U.S. Naval Academy and made one of the few speeches of the weekend. It was a eulogy, within which I tried to combine a sense of humor with the solemnity of the occasion. Of the 809 members of our graduating class, 201 were deceased. It was a time of some sadness, but Rosalynn and I had a great time with other seventy-year-olds who still knew how to enjoy themselves and seemed determined to avoid letting old age get the better of them. It is interesting to realize that thirteen of the twenty-six members of my rural high school graduating class have died, the higher mortality rate perhaps due to a lower average income and less access to effective medical care.

Perhaps the most troubling aspect of our later years is the need to face the inevitability of our own impending physical death. For some people, this fact becomes a cause of great distress, sometimes with attendant resentment against God or even those around us.

There are a lot of medical problems that concern us as we approach old age, but cancer is a special case for me and many others. Even as the eldest son, I am the only surviving member of my family. Except for my mother, all of them died at a relatively early age. My father died when he was fifty-nine, my oldest sister at sixty-four, my youngest sister when she was fifty-four, and my brother at fifty-one. All of them enjoyed cigarettes and all died with pancreatic cancer. Since fewer than one person in a thousand dies of this disease, I have accepted the presumption that my family has a genetic inclination toward pancreatic cancer, and I have regular blood tests and periodic CAT or MRI scans to help with early detection of this almost invariably fatal disease.

This has been a personal challenge to me for the past twenty years. The consensus is that the test results have been favorable so far, probably because I am the only one who has not smoked. I know from experience that a physician's advice concerning personal habits, diet, and exercise might help us avoid cancer, and a good physical examination can detect cancer of the skin, breast, cervix, colon, and prostate early enough for successful treatment.

If our doctors tell us that we have a terminal illness and can expect to live only another year, or five years, how would we respond? In fact, we confront exactly the same question if we are still healthy and have a life expectancy of fifteen or twenty more years. As our thoughts and attitudes are forced into a reorientation of priorities, we can change our focus from transient things to those that have a permanent importance and will never be lost.

During our final years (or months) of life, the

"important" things for which we may have struggled all our lives, mostly involving making money, tend to fade into relative insignificance. Some that we may have ignored or postponed during our earlier years, usually personal relationships, tend to become paramount.

As distressing as the prospect is, both spouses need to prepare for some final time—perhaps years—without the other. Chances are that a wife will survive her husband, a premise borne out by both statistics and my own personal observations.

For every one hundred American women there are only seventy men at age seventy, fifty men at age eighty, and just forty men at age eighty-five. These ratios were brought home to me a few years ago. At a Christmas party of the Plains Lions Club, a door prize was given to the one who could guess most closely how many widows and widowers lived in our town. Most of us named the two widowers but were surprised that there were fifty-one widows!

Because of the innate attractiveness of marriage in our society, there are many romances and remarriages among older people, even those in their eighties. They can be just as genuine and gratifying as those of younger couples, but studies have shown that there is one significant difference: Older people remarry primarily for companionship, often retaining a good portion of their own personal independence, with more limited commitments and often less personal intimacy than in early marriages.

We can either face death with fear, anguish, and unnecessary distress among those around us or, through faith and courage, confront the inevitable with equanimity, good humor, and peace. When other members of my family realized that they had a terminal illness, the finest medical care was available to them. But each chose to forgo elaborate artificial life-support systems and, with a few friends and family members at their bedside, they died peacefully. All of them retained their lifelong character and their personal dignity. During the final days of their lives they continued to enjoy themselves as well as possible and to reduce the suffering and anguish of those who survived. My older sister Gloria was surrounded by her biker friends and talked about Harley-Davidsons and their shared pleasures on the road. Her funeral cortege, in fact, was a hearse preceded by thirty-seven Harley-Davidson motorcycles. Until the end, my brother Billy and my mother retained their superb sense of humor, and my youngest sister, Ruth, was stalwart in her faith as an evangelist.

Rosalynn and I hope to follow in their footsteps, and we have signed living wills that will preclude the artificial prolongation of our lives.

10

What Is
Successful Aging?

Go out on a limb.
That's where the fruit is.

What should be our major goals as we prepare for our later years? You may be surprised to learn that I think one of the most important should be our own happiness. I don't consider this to be a selfish approach, because it will almost inevitably open up better relationships with others. It should be clear that happiness doesn't come automatically, but is something for which we must strive forthrightly, enthusiastically, and with imagination. We will fail if we just set a selfish goal: "I'm going to be happy!" So what is involved in enjoying our later years? I have read many studies that attempt to give us the answer.

Some sociologists have decided that the three most significant predictors of successful aging are (1) the level of education we have attained, (2) the amount of physical activity that we maintain, and (3) the degree of control that we feel we have over our own destiny. All these are important, but I don't agree that these are the ultimate criteria. For instance, let's assume that two men equally confident about their power to affect their own lives—a lonely college professor who runs five miles every day and a retired farmer who never attended college but has a cohesive and loving family and whose most strenuous exercise is hugging his wife several times a day. It is unlikely that the professor is either more successful or happier than the farmer.

Others believe that happiness depends on one or more good personal relationships and some involvement with a faith community, and the ability to extract from memories the positive things that give a sense of pride or at least the satisfaction of a worthy life. These are also good, but inadequate.

I'm inclined to agree with an elaborate study sponsored by the MacArthur Foundation, which concluded that the three indicators of successful aging are (1) avoiding disease and disability, (2) maintaining mental and physical function, and (3) continuing engagement with life. The latter involves keeping up relationships with others and performing productive activities. This engagement in living—successful adjustment to the changing conditions we have to face—will inevitably involve us with responsibilities, challenges, difficulties, and perhaps pain. But these experiences will tend to keep us closer to others and allow us to develop more self-respect and mastery over our own lives—crucial elements for a good life.

Sigmund Freud summarized all these propositions by saying that the essentials of human life are work and love. These are much closer to my own beliefs, providing we can provide an adequate definition for both words.

We tend to feel that our work defines who we are. In our later years, if we are asked, "Tell me about yourself," we might respond, "I'm retired," and perhaps go on to explain what we used to be. At different times in my life I have introduced myself as a submariner, farmer, warehouseman, state senator, governor, or even president, if that was necessary. I might have added where I lived, but that was about it. Now, even though not holding a steady job, I could reply, depending on my audience, that I am a professor, author, fly fisherman, or woodworker. I could add American, southerner, Christian, married, or grandfather. The point is that each of us is a complex human being, with multiple choices of our primary interests or identification at any moment. Keeping a number of these options alive is a good indication of the vitality of our existence.

I think most of us who grew up on farms during the Great Depression have been stamped for life by the experience. We saw many neighboring families lose their farms and homes because of excessive ambition, the purchase of new equipment, planting too large an acreage, or not tending well what was planted. The fear of bad weather and the resulting inability to pay our crop mortgage was constant. We learned to live very cautiously.

My concepts of life were shaped by these memories, even when I had a secure job as a naval officer. I was extremely careful about the future. Our gross income was only $300 a month when I was on my first ship, but I bought a $50 savings bond and paid the maximum national service life insurance premium permitted, and we increased our savings rate as my salary was slowly raised. We didn't buy an automobile until I became a submariner, and then we committed all my hazardous-duty pay to reduce this debt as rapidly as possible.

Later, when I resigned from the navy late in 1953, we qualified to live in a government housing project, where the rent was $31 a month. We used our small savings to invest in farm supplies to be sold in the Plains community. A severe drought in our area limited our total income to $280 during our first year in business, most of which was in unpaid customer accounts. Perhaps understandably, the local banks all refused to give me a loan to begin another year. Carter's Warehouse survived because our fertilizer supplier agreed to let me keep a small inventory if I paid them after I collected for the sales we made. We developed a profitable business during the following years, but I don't remember ever discussing at that time any plan for financial security in our old age, except that we would continue working as long as Rosalynn and I were physically able.

Instead of acting boldly and expanding my

personal horizons, I was more inclined to concentrate on existing duties, do them well, and make cautious and incremental changes in my life's commitments.

One Sunday I taught a Bible lesson that really perplexed me, in that it violated the basic philosophy of our farming community. It was from Ecclesiastes: "Whoever watches the wind will not plant; whoever looks at the cloud will not reap." We had been taught to watch the wind and clouds, and always to accommodate the weather in planting, cultivating, and harvesting. As I tried to explain the text to my class, I finally realized that the writer was saying, "Don't be too cautious; take a chance! If you wait for perfect conditions, you may end up living a timid and diminished life. The prospect of failure always exists, and it is painful and often embarrassing when we do fail. But it's better to fail while striving for something adventurous and uncertain than to say, 'I won't try, because I may not succeed completely.'"

It wasn't much later that, perhaps influenced by these thoughts, I decided to run for the state senate. Like anyone else, I certainly failed sometimes when I took chances—in the navy, in business, and in politics. But I learned that even the failures force us to stretch our hearts and minds, and the successes more than compensate for the losses. This premise is particularly applicable to those of us who have reached retirement age. It is a time when we can, by default, live a passive and inactive life. But there is a wonderful, if riskier, alternative. We can take advantage of our newfound freedom and embark on new and exciting adventures. We now have time to fulfill some earlier ambitions. If we make a mistake, there are plenty of fallbacks. We need not be too cautious.

11

Great Things for Ourselves

We worry too much about something to live on—
and too little about something to live for.

Most older people, once we are reasonably comfortable and secure, are inclined to want gratifying experiences rather than more belongings. It's impossible to list all the interesting opportunities that are available to almost any senior citizen. Let me mention just a few that Rosalynn and I have observed ourselves.

ADULT STUDIES

For more than fifteen years I have been a professor at Emory University, lecturing in almost every field, including medicine, anthropology, theology, journalism, creative writing, business, political science, and history. Most of my students are in their late teens or early twenties, but there are also several thousand older people who take advantage of classes at the university.

The latest issue of *Evening at Emory,* the bulletin listing the university's evening courses, offers new skills in painting, guitar, acting, negotiation, living alone, foreign languages, fly fishing, aikido, yoga, personal investments, fiction writing, genealogy, casting, and art appreciation. There are also discussion groups entitled "The Meaning of Life," "Starting Over After the Death of a Spouse," "Assertiveness Training," and "Career Assessment." All of these were on the list for just one Monday night! For those not near a great university, vocational-technical schools offer courses on travel, cooking, interior design, conflict resolution, financial management, piano by ear, auto repair, horticulture, photography, and furniture making.

We often have groups of happy senior citizens visit our town or our church. They are participating in Elderhostel, a wonderful organization that offers continuing travel and learning experiences to hundreds of thousands of retired people at a very low cost. These visitors, all retired, have either driven down from a university in Atlanta or are studying at nearby Georgia Southwestern State University and spending a few days at the international headquarters of Habitat for Humanity. For information, consult their Web site: http://www.elderhostel.org/EHORG/.

TALKING BOOKS

No matter what our present interests are or past literary habits have been, talking books (sometimes called audio books or books on tape) are a wonderful supplement to our regular reading. I have recorded several of my books, and I receive many letters from older citizens, others who are partially blind, and people of all ages who listen while jogging or riding in an automobile. When we go on trips with our grandchildren, we always have a collection of audio books on hand. Almost all libraries provide this service, and for those with poor eyesight, free tape players and an almost unlimited supply of talking books are available.

FAMILY HISTORY

One of Rosalynn's favorite suggestions is for older people to tape-record a history of one's life and family. It's better when younger relatives ask the questions. We know how much we value the interviews we did twenty years ago with our mothers and my uncle Buddy.

CLEAN OUT OR CHANGE THE HOUSE

A good project is just to clean out the house! Most of us older people will remember Fibber McGee's closet, and we're likely to have similar places at home. Sorting through forgotten objects will bring back fond memories, provide possibilities for contributions to charity, and make available new space for a woodshop, an artist's studio, a hothouse, or more bookshelves.

GET AWAY FROM IT ALL

The home we built in Plains in 1961 is still intact, but we've modified it several times. Our original garage is now my office, Rosalynn works in a bedroom that used to belong to one of our boys, and our back porch has been glassed in to make it part of the interior. We did one other thing that was more ambitious and costly: With another couple, we split the costs of building a log cabin alongside a trout stream in north Georgia. While I was writing my presidential memoir I designed and built the beds, chairs, tables, and chifforobes with which it is furnished. We get there a few times each year, and it's a favorite place for our children and grandchildren.

ADVENTURES

It's also good to capitalize on our friendships to arrange some unorthodox, inexpensive, and interesting adventures. One that I'll always remember is a day we spent on a shrimp boat in our Atlantic coastal waters. In addition to marveling over the assortment of creatures that the net produced, we learned about the lives and occupations of some of our Georgia neighbors.

THE INTERNET

Readers will have a different list of things to do, depending on their interests. During the last few years there has evolved a wonderful opportunity for people of all ages to explore literature, art, news, and places, to make new friends, and to communicate with any organization or acquaintance instantly—all from our own homes! This is, of course, the Internet, which almost anyone (not just young people) can learn to use in a few hours. All it takes is a modest investment in equipment and a willingness to take a brief introductory course, available in almost every American community.

12

Seniors Can Do Great Things for Others

*When it comes to giving,
some people will stop at nothing.*

There are a lot of interesting things we can do that are helpful to other people. One is to work with a political campaign—or even seek office ourselves! Don't forget that we elderly are quite a strong voting bloc. Individuals can visit shut-ins, join in local community projects, or volunteer as described later in this chapter. Most faith congregations have organized projects, some of them quite innovative. One example that I like is helpful to senior citizens. With a relatively simple automatic telephone dialer, each morning a church calls several dozen people living alone. If they answer, that's the end of it; if not, someone visits the home to see if there is anything wrong.

A village in the Catskills was plagued, as are many communities, with accumulated litter along the streets and highways. A doctor's wife decided to do the simplest thing possible to correct the problem: She went out every afternoon and picked up the trash. Others saw her, and Scouts, civic clubs, and religious congregations soon joined her. The woman's town became one of the cleanest in America. Any senior can do the same thing.

One of our societal mistakes is the failure to measure or even to acknowledge the tremendous contribution that retired people make to our nation. Labor statistics compiled by our government agencies are based only on what is done for pay, excluding the same (or more beneficial) work done within one's own home or as voluntary service to others. People who spin roulette wheels or do striptease dances are considered to be productive, but not people who care for a disabled friend or family member or do volunteer work in a hospital. Homemakers are not included in government records as productive workers, but if my neighbor and I would agree to clean each other's house and pay each other for the work, then both would be counted as adding to our gross national product. This statistical policy greatly underestimates the work of all Americans, but especially women and older people. The fact is that in every decade after age fifty-five, unpaid work is the main form of productive activity for both men and women, and yet statistics overlook this and create a serious impression of idleness.

There is still a tremendous potential to expand the present level of volunteerism among elders. Although more than 80 percent of us do work around our homes and 70 percent provide some assistance to friends and relatives, relatively few retirees volunteer for other kinds of service. Two out of three older people do none, and most active volunteers contribute less than four hours a week.

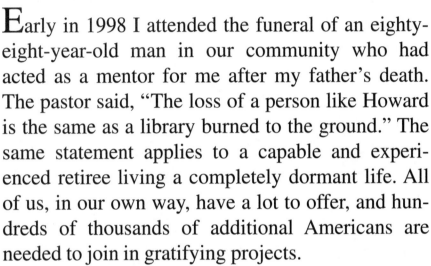

Early in 1998 I attended the funeral of an eighty-eight-year-old man in our community who had acted as a mentor for me after my father's death. The pastor said, "The loss of a person like Howard is the same as a library burned to the ground." The same statement applies to a capable and experienced retiree living a completely dormant life. All of us, in our own way, have a lot to offer, and hundreds of thousands of additional Americans are needed to join in gratifying projects.

Rosalynn and I are active in Habitat for Humanity, raising funds and going each year to a different site to help build at least one home for a family in need. We work side by side with the family and with other volunteers, beginning our work on Monday morning with just a concrete slab and finishing on Friday with a completed and landscaped home. During the same week, from twenty to a hundred other homes are completed in the same project, with an average of thirty workers per house. Some of the volunteers have joined us for each of the last fourteen years and continue their Habitat work during other weeks when homes are built at a more normal pace. Many volunteers are older than we; some are in their late eighties and even early nineties.

There are other organizations that are equally interesting but require less physical effort. When I first became president, Rosalynn and I helped to organize the Friendship Force, based on an inspired idea of a former Presbyterian missionary named Wayne Smith. The concept was to have groups of Americans travel to other nations, stay for a week or two in private homes, learn as much as possible about the foreign community, and then welcome their hosts for a reciprocal visit to this country. Since then, more than two million people have participated, and Friendship Force organizations now exist throughout America and in more than fifty nations.

The majority of these goodwill ambassadors are between sixty-five and seventy-five years old. Kay Lanz, now eighty-five, has visited thirty-five countries. My mother went to Ireland with a group from Iowa when she was seventy-nine, and Rosalynn's mother, Allie, made a similar visit to England at about the same age. Her group was in Durham Cathedral when Queen Elizabeth II came there for a visit. The queen noticed the Americans, stopped to question them, and Mrs. Allie explained the Friendship Force concept to her.

In 1984 I visited Hiroshima and made a speech about peace and nuclear arms control to several thousand people at "ground zero." Afterward, when I went into the atomic bomb museum nearby, some Friendship Force volunteers told me that they had arranged an exchange of visits between families who were living in Hiroshima and Pearl Harbor when their communities were bombed! During these kinds of exchanges, intense friendships are formed. Now there are about ten overseas visits a month, usually involving two weeks of warmhearted home-stay and various side trips to learn about the country. The average cost is less than a normal round-trip airline ticket—about $1,000 to Europe or Central America, $1,800 to Japan, and $3,000 to South Africa (which includes a visit to a game park). One of the most popular regions is New Zealand and Australia, with costs beginning at about $1,700 from the West Coast. Special exchanges are often arranged between people who share the same interests: teachers, lawyers, farmers, and even zoo docents.

For more information, phone 404-522-9490, or consult their Web site at www.friendship-force.org.

When Rosalynn and I found that our business in Plains was growing rapidly and becoming more complicated, we needed advice from an experienced manager. On the advice of our local banker, we called on the National Senior Service Corps, and the retired vice president of a major automobile parts company drove down from Atlanta to spend several days with us. He gave us practical instruction in the handling of personnel, inventories, accounts receivable, and the best ways to plan for the further expansion of Carter's Warehouse. Later, while monitoring an election in Nicaragua, we found international volunteer executives there in the rural areas, helping to reorganize the production, ginning, and marketing of the nation's cotton crop following the destruction of the Contra war.

There are more than half a million part-time older workers in the National Senior Service Corps. Twenty-four thousand seniors now work as foster grandparents, and twelve thousand help older neighbors with bills, shopping, and local transportation, as well as provide care for those suffering from strokes, diabetes, and Alzheimer's (for a tenth of the cost of nursing home care). Others, known as Seniors for Schools, put in at least fifteen hours a week to help parents and teachers guarantee that children in low-income neighborhoods learn how to read and write. Nearly another half million retired and senior volunteers carry out other tasks such as teaching English to immigrants and helping communities suffering from natural disasters. In July 1994 the Plains area was inundated with a flood that caused thirty-one deaths and destroyed thousands of homes. Now, three and a half years later, organized groups of senior volunteers from many states are still working to help our neighbors repair their devastated lives. To get involved, phone 202-606-5000, or look up www.cns.gov.

Because of the generally aging population, better health, and the tight job market, the number of older workers has increased an amazing 65 percent in the last decade. Many need to supplement retirement benefits and are not satisfied with a relatively inert life at home. Employers find them attractive to hire because they are usually cheaper, require lower benefits, are dependable, experienced, easy to train, and are often eager to take on new skills.

The Retired Senior Volunteer Program (RSVP) has chapters in many cities, and provides training and placement for senior volunteers. There are even part-time jobs available for senior citizens in the federal government. Just one example is the Environmental Protection Agency's Senior Environmental Employment (SEE) program, now in thirty locations nationwide. Averaging sixty-seven years of age, workers are not allowed to replace full-time civil servants, but put in twenty hours a week in a range of jobs from clerical occupations to advanced work in engineering and science. For information, phone 202-331-5017.

Other employment policies are changing because many working people want to spend more time with their families and less on the job, while others just desire more scheduling options. One experimental proposal being tested in America is to use four hours as a "work module" instead of the usual eight hours. This provides greater flexibility for employers and employees, at the same time permitting the packaging of two modules together for those employers who wish to retain the standard eight-hour work period. This approach has worked on factory assembly lines, for secretaries, nurses, librarians, and business executives, and within a growing number of government agencies.

13

Some Remarkable
Old People

*It's better to be seventy years young
than forty years old.*

A lot of senior citizens ask, "What can I do at my age?" This implies either that we are too old to remain very active or that we don't have any ideas about interesting or helpful things to do. I'd like to give a few examples of interesting seniors who have affected my life and whose experiences may help to answer the question.

MY MOTHER

There is a big difference between getting older and growing old. When my father died, in 1953, Mama was fifty-five, past retirement age for most registered nurses. For a few weeks she played the expected role of a grieving widow, but then decided that there was more to life than staying at home and enjoying a passive existence. She continued to age for thirty more years but never grew old.

Taking on a completely new life, she worked first as housemother to ninety-five wild Kappa Alpha fraternity students at Auburn University. For six years she was their protector, confidante, loan and bail officer, and personal counselor. For most of them, she was a more intimate and understanding friend than their parents.

Then, to accommodate some friends, she agreed to open and manage their new nursing home in Blakely, Georgia, about a hundred miles south of Plains. After a few years she became tired of "being with old folks" and came back home. She soon saw a television advertisement for Peace Corps volunteers that declared there was no age limit. At sixty-eight she finished her training and was sent to a small town near Bombay, India, where she served for two years. After that, Mama made more than five hundred speeches describing her experiences and encouraging her audiences not to let old age be a limit on their lives. At the age of eighty-five she was still full of life, never failing to wake up in the morning with determination to make the new day an adventure.

VOLUNTEERS AT THE CARTER CENTER

We have almost 150 invaluable volunteers who work at The Carter Center, opening, routing, and answering the thousands of letters we receive each month, giving guided tours to school groups and other visitors, landscaping, and acting as docents. At the time of this writing, twenty-six are in their sixties, twenty-four are in their seventies, six are in their eighties, and two are more than ninety. Two women, both in their eighties, typify our workers. Sylvia Eizenstat works more than six hundred hours each year and hosts some of the more prestigious guests. Oleta Entrekin drives eighty miles to the center twice a week and conducts group tours of the center and the presidential library.

I was surprised to learn that our volunteers offer their services to many other organizations, including the state child abuse center, the diabetes association, the United Way, The Martin Luther King, Jr. Center, City of Hope, and the Society of Retired Executives. They also volunteer in Atlanta's local hospitals, serve in poverty areas, help their churches and synagogues, teach computer and dancing classes, work in political campaigns, and help build houses with Habitat for Humanity.

SISSY

A person who demonstrates vividly how the citizen of a community can live a full and productive life is my aunt, Emily Visscher, universally known as Sissy. In her hometown of Roswell, Sissy has been a driving force in the women's club, the garden club, the historical society, and the recreation commission, and was an organizer of the League of Women Voters. Sissy traveled extensively in many nations with the Atlanta Boy Choir, as chaperone and surrogate mother to the members while they were away from home. She also served as assistant to the chaplain of Northside Hospital and as an elder in the Presbyterian Church. At eighty-one, several years after the death of her husband, she married a widower with whom she shares a full and exciting life of travel and volunteer work. Before retiring at the age of eighty-five, she coordinated the work of the volunteers who serve at The Carter Center.

ADMIRAL RICKOVER

With the exception of my father, Admiral Hyman Rickover is the man who has had the greatest effect on my life. He was born in Poland in 1900, came to America as a child, and was graduated from the U.S. Naval Academy in 1922. His remarkable intellect and dedication moved him quickly into the program that developed the world's first use of atomic power for peaceful uses, the production of electricity and the propulsion of ships.

I went to work for him in 1951 and was placed in charge of building the nuclear power plant that would go into the second atomic submarine, the U.S.S. *Sea Wolf*. The first was the *Nautilus*, which used water to cool the reactor core. Our power plant used liquid sodium for this purpose. Both designs worked well, but it was later decided that the water-cooled plants were safer and could provide uniformity.

I resigned from the navy before the *Sea Wolf* was commissioned, but later, while I was president,

Rosalynn and I went out with the admiral during the sea trials of one of our newest submarines. He let us control its course, speed, and depth, and described in detail all its features and the responsibilities of each member of the crew. He had helped design, build, and man enough nuclear-powered ships to extend for ten miles if aligned in a row with bows touching sterns. Despite the highly experimental nature of some of them, there had never been a fatal accident caused by a failure of any of his power plants.

In addition to the highest naval honors, he was given the rare Congressional Medal of Honor for his work, and I was honored to award him the Presidential Medal of Freedom. At age eighty-two, Rickover was still in full charge of the U.S. Navy's nuclear power program and resented it very much when he was forced to retire by President Ronald Reagan (who was not much younger at the time.)

D.W. BROOKS

One of the most remarkable men I've known is D.W. Brooks, who was born in 1901 in Royston, Georgia, also the home of Ty Cobb. As a professor at the University of Georgia, D.W. saw the ravages of the Great Depression and realized that the dirt farmers of Georgia were at the complete mercy of bankers, merchants, buyers, and wild swings in the price of farm produce that always seemed at variance with the farmers' needs. He organized an agricultural cooperative that quickly became one of the largest in the world, and later a mutual insurance company, whose members finally had some voice in their own destiny. A master of global markets, D.W. was a valued adviser for Presidents Truman, Eisenhower, Kennedy, Johnson, and Ford, and for me. Both mentally and physically acute in his nineties, he is still receiving distinguished honors for his ongoing work as a statesman, a Christian, and a champion for the "little people." He is especially revered among the African-American citizens of the South.

I have spent hours with D.W. in a boat since he turned ninety, competing unsuccessfully with him in catching bass on a fly rod. All of his hunting companions have marveled at his sustained prowess as a wing shot, whether the quarry is doves or quail. In his ninety-fifth year he continued to escort a group of his friends to Alaska for an annual fishing expedition, holding his own with others a third his age. A delightful raconteur, D.W. is one of the best examples I know of a man who maintains interest and purpose in life and enjoys strong ties with hundreds of his friends.

ESTHER PETERSON

In a 1966 issue of *Time* magazine, President Lyndon Johnson credited sixty-year-old Esther Peterson, a partner of Eleanor Roosevelt, with bringing about a new era for the American consumer. Eleven years later she agreed to be my special White House assistant for consumer affairs. I was proud to award her the Presidential Medal of Freedom because she "made sure that the average American is not cheated, that they are told the truth, treated fairly, and can have some inner sense of trust in the free enterprise system."

A dear friend, she was sitting beside me on a couch when I was nominated as the Democratic candidate for president. After she and I left the White House, she worked for the United Nations to establish international rules that prevent the sale of toxic and dangerous materials, banned in the United States, to unsuspecting people in the developing world. She didn't think it was right to sell flammable clothing to African children or to ship drums of poisonous chemicals to be stacked in their neighborhoods. At ninety-one she was still a driving force in protecting women, the elderly, minorities, and hundreds of millions of consumers who would never know her.

RIOICHI SASAKAWA AND NORMAN BORLAUG

One of the people who have helped change my life's work was a Japanese philanthropist named Rioichi Sasakawa. He was a fighter pilot during World War II, and was imprisoned for three years after the Japanese surrendered, but never charged or put on trial. He devised in his prison cell a plan to help his country recover from its devastating defeat, and when finally released he put it into effect. He built a number of lakes around the nation, and hundreds of identical speedboats so that races could be staged and people could bet on the outcome. Although the idea was at first controversial, all the betting profit went into a foundation that rebuilt Japan's shipbuilding industry. Later, with great personal influence over hundreds of millions of dollars, Mr. Sasakawa began dozens of humanitarian projects around the globe.

In 1981 he came to my home in Plains. His first

remark was, "I never dreamed that a president of the United States would live in such a modest place!" His second comment was more welcome: "I hear you are establishing a center to do good things for peace and human rights, and I want to give you a half million dollars to help with the project." That started a beautiful partnership, and we were able to see his projects in almost every country we visited. In rich nations he provided for exchanges of thousands of college students; in poor ones he furnished homes for lepers and their children and paid for much-needed health programs.

In 1985, when Rioichi Sasakawa was eighty-six, together we commenced a program to teach small-scale farmers in Africa how to increase dramatically their production of basic food grains, including corn, rice, wheat, sorghum, and millet. I would negotiate a contract with the president of the nation and all his key cabinet officers.

Nobel laureate Norman Borlaug, who won the Nobel Peace Prize in 1970 for bringing a "green revolution" to India and Pakistan, is the leading scientist in this program. He would send an agricultural specialist into the country to train hundreds of extension workers, and Sasakawa would provide the funding. Now eighty-four, Borlaug is still going strong and is regularly in the fields of

Ghana, Ethiopia, Mali, Burkina Faso, Mozambique, and seven other nations. We now have about six hundred thousand farmers in our program in twelve African nations, and they regularly triple their production.

UNCLE BUDDY

One subtle measurement of life's quality is the degree of interest we have in things outside ourselves. My mother constantly explored every aspect of life, and so did my father's brother, whom we called Uncle Buddy. He ran a country store in Plains and was one of the largest mule traders in Georgia. When I would come home on leave from the navy, most members of my family would make a few perfunctory inquiries about life on a submarine, but my uncle would ask questions for a couple of hours. How many men were on board? Did each have his own bunk? Did they have three meals a day? How big was the kitchen? What happened if someone had claustrophobia? Could the officers punish the men? Where did we get fresh water? How did we know where we were? Could we see or hear whales? Why did we need submarines? How did we hope to win a battle? At the age of ninety he was still like this with almost everyone who came into his store, always adding new dimensions to his own life and making his visitors feel important.

All of these people were active in their eighties and nineties, either continuing a long career or seeking new things to do. Some of them became famous because of their extraordinary work, and others were just ordinary folks whose achievements were equally successful.

14

A Successful
Life

*Too many folks spend their lives
aging rather than maturing.*

A recent *USA Today* poll showed that Americans
consider the six top measurements of success to be
satisfaction with life, being in control, a good marriage, being good at one's job, the ability to afford
important things, and successful children. Less than
25 percent said that "a lot of money" signified success. The first two are closely related, so being in
control of our lives is the foremost consideration.
What are the steps in reaching this source of success? Psychologists say they are (1) conceiving our
important goals, (2) focusing on things we can control, (3) fixing one problem at a time, (4) dividing

long-term goals into manageable parts, and (5) being satisfied with small steps.

Retirement years are a time to define, or redefine, a successful life, both in retrospect and for our remaining years—a definition likely to be quite different from that of our younger years.

After a certain time in life, most of us have already made some of our most troubling decisions, such as the choice of a profession and a life mate, how to achieve our goals in competition with others, and perhaps how to raise our children. A large bank account, a beautiful and prominent home, eminence in our profession, and seeing our name in the society columns tend to become our ambitions in life. There is nothing wrong with these things, but some of us become disappointed or frustrated when we have failed to be "successful" by achieving them. The fact is that our legitimate human ambitions often cause us the anger, envy, suffering, pain, frustration, and sense of inadequacy that deprive us of inner peace and joy.

It is a sign of maturity when we can accept honestly and courageously that frustrated dreams, illness, disability, and eventual death are all normal facets of a person's existence—and that despite these, we can still continue to learn, grow, and adopt challenging goals.

Being a good citizen is a measure of success and

123

a worthy goal, but it's not enough. I can obey all the legal codes and still lose the potential for a full life. Criminal laws set minimum standards, within which our governments attempt to guarantee our rights and prohibit harm or injury to others. Some laws also try to prevent self-imposed injury, such as by mandating seat belts and motorcycle helmets, limiting smoking areas, or prohibiting the use of certain narcotics. But none of them requires us to be kind, generous, or forgiving, or to have a good relationship with other people. The laws help us, but they don't set the most important parameters of a good life, nor do they establish the highest moral or ethical standards.

Suppose we have every material thing we need, plus a good education, a stable family, physical and mental ability, and some good hobbies. For many people, that's *still* not enough. Within each successful and happy life there also needs to be some concept of greatness, some superb example to follow, something on which we can always depend, something that is inspirational, exalting, transcendent. We need to explore the maximum capabilities we have—to search for ways to challenge ourselves, to stretch our minds and our hearts. At the same time, we also need a haven within which we can find friendship, encouragement, answers to questions about life, and the assurance of assistance when we confront crises or tragedies.

The transcendent goal for a Christian is emulation of the life of Christ. A basic belief of Judaism is that people are defined by the ability to make an ethical choice based on a covenant relationship with God. Supreme ideals for Moslems are comprehension of the Koran, growth in self-awareness, and compatibility with the world around us. Confucius emphasized contemplation, self-revelation, and good living in every stage of existence, with self-discipline and beneficence to others as common aims. He taught that in youth we must guard against lust, in middle age against strife (aggressive acts to reach personal goals), and in old age avarice (clinging to what we have, including life itself). The Japanese emphasize the seasons of the year and tend to equate them with the seasons of life, with each bringing its unique attractions. Their ultimate objective is to improve one's ability to perform assigned duties, leading to inner tranquillity, particularly during one's later years. The slogan of sumo wrestlers is a summation of this philosophy: "To be great is to be equal to the task."

I think that, regardless of our culture, age, or even personal handicaps, we can still strive for something exceptional. Why not expand our sights instead of restricting our lives and accepting the lowest common denominator of a dormant existence? Faith, either in God or in ourselves, will permit us to take a chance on a new path, perhaps different from the one we now follow. It may be surprising where it leads.

15

Simple Things Are the Most Important

Finding a way to live the simple life is
today's most complicated problem.

Retirement is a time to change our previous ambitions and concentrate on things of more immediate interest to us, seemingly simple things. It is very likely that these are the most important things of all, encompassing our most cherished desires and perhaps the closest relationships we've ever had with other people, including our children, grandchildren, and friends and neighbors.

One of our most important goals might be to perfect what will probably be our final dwelling place, whether it is an old family home with a garden or a new condominium in a sunny climate. As a navy couple, we moved frequently, so when we built our present house in Plains, it was our sixteenth residence. Since then we've had government housing in Atlanta and Washington. One of the things we've learned during this relatively nomadic life is that where we lived didn't have much effect on our personal happiness. We had an almost unlimited choice of retirement homes when we left the White House. My professorship was at Emory University, and our major work would be at The Carter Center, so Atlanta was the most logical option.

Despite some serious reservations, we came back to Plains, basing our final decision on apparently simple personal interests that we considered most important. Plains was the home of our ancestors, where we had strong ties to our families, our neighbors, and our land. In a relatively isolated town of about seven hundred, though, what was there to do? In fact, we've found plenty to keep us busy in Plains, through community improvement projects, our churches, the historical society, social events, sports, annual festivals, and even drama productions.

We especially like the close-knit relationship among our citizens. Whenever a family is in trouble, the community moves into action, and we join together to raise funds if there are serious financial needs. The churches are the center of life for almost all of us. Even with our small population, we have eight active congregations inside the city limits. Three are Baptist, two Methodist, and a Lutheran, Church of Christ, and Church of God. There are four other churches within three miles of town.

Our biggest community project has involved every family—and almost everyone who has ever lived here. The old Plains High School building had sheltered all three of our sons, both Rosalynn and me, and even her mother, more than seventy-five years ago, but had been abandoned and was rapidly becoming a dilapidated eyesore. With country music concerts, annual carnivals, cake sales, and direct-mail appeals to high school alumni, we raised $2 million to match U.S. Park Service funds. As a historical site, the building has now been renovated and a remarkable museum installed in it to let today's students and teachers learn how classes were conducted in an American rural community in the 1930s. More than 10 percent of our total population performed this year in a pageant at the newly renovated auditorium.

Based on our own experience, it seems that almost any community can provide interesting and gratifying opportunities if we're willing to explore what's going on around us and to become involved.

One of the most interesting and gratifying responsibilities at our age is to decide what to do with accumulated wealth and possessions. In all too many cases, couples fail to leave a will of any kind. Whether it's a few pieces of furniture and some personal items or broader holdings of stocks and real estate, we should decide what will happen to our belongings. We must remember that, no matter what we do, the Internal Revenue Service will be one of our major heirs. How much of our estate will go for taxes can be greatly affected by whether or not we plan for the future.

Although it has been something of a chore, Rosalynn and I have developed careful plans for the proper distribution of what we own. Our first task has been to meet the needs of whichever of us survives the other. Then, with the advice of experts on tax laws and estate planning, we have made current annual gifts and future provisions for other members of our family. We are leaving a substantial portion of our estate to The Carter Center, where we have worked for the past fifteen years, to perpetuate

its good works. Through a charitable-gift annuity, our friends and supporters can make a gift to The Carter Center and still receive regular and increased income, take an immediate tax deduction, and reduce capital gains and estate taxes. There are other opportunities for planned-gift donors, whom we consider to be partners in everything we do.

We have retained an interest in some of our bequests, amending the arrangements to accommodate changing circumstances and sometimes for sentimental reasons. For instance, we have a special feeling about our property around Plains. Both Rosalynn's and my ancestors who were born in the 1700s are buried there, and most of the land that we own was acquired several generations ago. We made our income from agriculture during the years after I left the navy, and we are intimately familiar with even our more remote fields and woodlands. We want to be careful about putting excessive conditions on its ownership, but at the same time we wish to keep it intact and owned by our direct descendants.

I've come to realize, especially in my later years, that *all* of us have adequate talent, intelligence, education, social status, and opportunity to be completely successful in life.

The simple things that comprise success include our own happiness, satisfaction, peace, joy, and sense of being worthy. We have available many sources of strength and wisdom, especially from our religions. As a Christian and a Bible teacher, I have found assurances that are important to me. How often do we feel perfectly satisfied with ourselves, filled with inner joy and peace? We are assured, "My peace I give you. . . . Don't let your heart be troubled." The promise is "peace, which passes all understanding," and to "rejoice with joy unspeakable and full of glory."

The Corinthians asked Saint Paul to define the things that were most important, with eternal significance. His response was somewhat mysterious: the things we cannot see.

What are these things?

I have kept biblical references to a minimum in this book, but I will make an exception for one beautiful passage in which Paul answered this question and put life's priorities in their proper perspective. Perhaps to the consternation of some deeply religious people, many of whom would answer the question with the word *faith,* Paul said, "If I have all faith, so as to move mountains, but do not have love, I am nothing." How about exceptional talent and intelligence? "Though I speak with the tongues of men and of angels . . . and have the gift of prophecy, and understand all mysteries, and all knowledge," they are superficial and meaningless without love. How about generosity, benevolence, or self-sacrifice? Paul says, "If I give away all my possessions, and if I give my body to be burned, but do not have love, I gain nothing."

What we cannot see are the component parts of love that Paul delineates: patience, kindness, truthfulness, hope, endurance, and generosity. These are the elements of success in life, common to almost all religions. How much wealth, fame, intelligence, education, or prestige do they require?

You might say, "It's good to quote beautiful verses of scripture, but how can it have any practical or positive effect on my life?" During the past seventy years or so I have experienced all kinds of love, including family affection as a child or parent, sexual or erotic love, and brotherly love or friendship. As C. S. Lewis explains, we would not be conceived without erotic love or nurtured without the affection of our parents. These are necessary for the perpetuation of the human race.

Friendship is quite different. Lewis says that eros is a sharing of naked bodies, while friendship is a sharing of personalities, which involves the relative isolation of two or more people from the crowd because of a shared trust or interest. With a friend we feel a special compatibility, often permitting a freedom of communication or understanding that does not exist with others, even one's own blood kin. The mutual feelings of friendship are rarely expressed to each other, although sometimes to others. "He is my friend" is a powerful statement.

There is a special blessing in camaraderie with others. For most of us, these relationships are all too rare. As a submariner, I felt close ties to a few shipmates, possibly because we realized that our lives were in each other's hands. Separation from our families during extended voyages helped to bind us together. There are still some longtime acquaintances whose very presence gives me a warm feeling and generates a natural smile on my face. I feel more relaxed and even eloquent in their presence.

Retirement offers us a chance to create new friendships and, perhaps more important, to renew and enjoy old ones. Recently Rosalynn and I spent a long weekend with two couples on the Eastern Shore of Maryland. Both of them had been deeply involved in my campaigns and administrations as governor and president. As we sat around a fire on a stormy November evening, we all agreed that we never would have had such an opportunity to enjoy each other's company during those earlier and busier days.

The three loves mentioned above all come naturally and are mutually advantageous, at least for a while. They may, perhaps, evolve into the ultimate kind, for which the Greek word is *agape*. This is love filled with unselfishness, grace, and forgiveness, with the happiness and well-being of other people preeminent.

The simple things—our own happiness, peace, joy, satisfaction, and the exploration of love in all its forms—are the key to the virtues of life, at any age.

You are old when regrets take the place of dreams.

Index

ABOUT THE AUTHOR

Jimmy Carter (James Earl Carter, Jr.), thirty-ninth president of the United States, was born October 1, 1924, in the small farming town of Plains, Georgia, and grew up in the nearby community of Archery. On July 7, 1946, he married Rosalynn Smith. In 1962 he won election to the Georgia Senate and became Georgia's seventy-sixth governor on January 12, 1971. He was elected president on November 2, 1976.

Jimmy Carter served as president from January 20, 1977, to January 20, 1981. Noteworthy foreign policy accomplishments of his administration included the Panama Canal treaties, the Camp David Accords, the treaty of peace between Egypt and Israel, the SALT II treaty with the Soviet Union, and the establishment of U.S. diplomatic relations with the People's Republic of China. He championed human rights throughout the world. On the domestic side, the administration's achievements included a comprehensive energy program conducted by a new Department of Energy; deregulation in energy, transportation, communications, and finance; major educational programs under a new Department of Education; and major environmental protection legislation, including the Alaska Lands Act.

President Carter is the author of thirteen previous books. In 1982 he became University Distinguished Professor at Emory University in Atlanta, Georgia, and founded The Carter Center, which addresses national and international issues of public policy and attempts to promote democracy, protect human rights, and prevent disease and other afflictions. In 1991, President Carter launched The Atlanta Project (TAP), a communitywide effort to attack the social problems associated with poverty.

President Carter has served on the board of directors, and he and Rosalynn are regular volunteers for Habitat for Humanity, a nonprofit organization that helps needy people in the United States and in other countries renovate and build homes for themselves. He also teaches Sunday school and is a deacon in the Maranatha Baptist Church of Plains. For recreation, he enjoys fly-fishing, woodworking, jogging, cycling, tennis, and skiing.

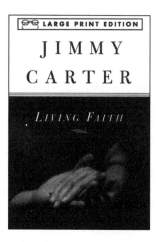
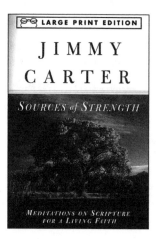

Look for these and other Random House Large Print books at your local bookstore

Angelou, Maya, *Even the Stars Look Lonesome*
Berendt, John, *Midnight in the Garden of Good and Evil*
Brinkley, David, *Everyone Is Entitled to My Opinion*
Carr, Caleb, *The Angel of Darkness*
Carter, Jimmy, *Living Faith*
Carter, Jimmy, *Sources of Strength*
Chopra, Deepak, *Ageless Body, Timeless Mind*
Chopra, Deepak, *The Path to Love*
Crichton, Michael, *Airframe*
Cronkite, Walter, *A Reporter's Life*
Daley, Rosie, *In the Kitchen with Rosie*
Flagg, Fannie, *Daisy Fay and the Miracle Man*
Flagg, Fannie, *Fried Green Tomatoes at the Whistle Stop Cafe*
Hepburn, Katharine, *Me*
Hiaasen, Carl, *Lucky You*
James, P. D., *A Certain Justice*
Koontz, Dean, *Sole Survivor*
Landers, Ann, *Wake Up and Smell the Coffee!*
le Carré, John, *The Tailor of Panama*
Lindbergh, Anne Morrow, *Gift from the Sea*
Mayle, Peter, *Chasing Cézanne*
Morrison, Toni, *Paradise*
Mother Teresa, *A Simple Path*
Patterson, Richard North, *Silent Witness*
Peck, M. Scott, M.D., *Denial of the Soul*
Phillips, Louis, editor, *The Random House Large Print Treasury of Best-Loved Poems*
Powell, Colin with Joseph E. Persico, *My American Journey*
Preston, Richard, *The Cobra Event*
Rampersad, Arnold, *Jackie Robinson*
Shaara, Jeff, *Gods and Generals*
Snead, Sam with Fran Pirozzolo, *The Game I Love*
Truman, Margaret, *Murder in the House*
Tyler, Anne, *Ladder of Years*
Updike, John, *Golf Dreams*
Weil, Andrew, M.D., *Eight Weeks to Optimum Health*